DATE DUE

DO WHATEVER HE TELLS YOU

Finding Joy
in Pleasing God

by Henry Libersat

St. Paul Books & Media

Imprimatur:
Most Reverend Thomas J. Grady
Bishop of Orlando
September 14, 1989

Library of Congress Cataloging-in-Publication Data
Libersat, Henry.
    Do whatever He tells you: finding joy in pleasing God / Henry
Libersat.
        p. cm.
    ISBN 0-8198-1819-4 : $7.95
    1. Spiritual life—Catholic authors.   2. God—Worship and love.
    3. Obedience—Religious aspects—Christianity.   4. Spiritual
    exercises. I. Title.
    BX2350.2.L4575 1990
    248.4'82—dc20   90-43483
                                                               CIP

Printed and published in the U.S.A. by St. Paul Books & Media,
50 St. Paul's Avenue, Boston, MA 02130.

St. Paul Books & Media is the publishing house of the Daughters of St. Paul,
an international congregation of women religious serving the Church with
the communications media.

1 2 3 4 5 6 7 8 9   98 97 96 95 94 93 92 91 90

To
Francis and Doris Meagher,
spiritual parents to hundreds,
whose love for God
has led them to live Mary's counsel
to
"Do whatever he tells you."

"On the third day there was a wedding at Cana in Galilee, and the mother of Jesus was there. Jesus and his disciples had likewise been invited to the celebration. At a certain point the wine ran out, and Jesus' mother told him, 'They have no more wine.' Jesus replied, 'Woman, how does this concern of yours involve me? My hour has not yet come.' His mother instructed those waiting on table, 'Do whatever he tells you'" (Jn. 2:1-5).

Contents

Foreword

Deacon Henry Libersat is an author who understands the human heart: its strengths, its sorrows, its glories and its griefs. In his latest book, Libersat opens his heart and reveals the secret of his own happiness.

The formula is simple and was revealed by Mary, the Mother of Jesus, at Cana in Galilee: "Do whatever he tells you."

Deacon Henry expands on the formula by offering solid, clear and persuasive explanations on how God's will is made manifest to us through the commandments, the Church, and most of all, through Jesus.

A very readable book with a personal touch.

Rev. Norm Muckerman, C.SS.R.
Retired Editor, *The Liguorian*
Past President, Catholic Press
Association

Thanks to . . .

- "Lady Margaret" (better known as Peg), my wife and best friend, for reading this manuscript, making valuable suggestions and always being there.

- Bert Ghezzi and Father John Catoir for sharing their reactions to the manuscript and for suggestions in better organizing the material.

- Bishop Thomas J. Grady for his imprimatur and Father Matthew J. Connolly of the Diocese of Orlando for reading this work for theological accuracy and pastoral sensitivity.

- To Toi Fitzpatrick of Lake Mary, FL, for her generous assistance in clerical work in producing this book—and three others in which I thoughtlessly forgot to mention her valuable help and generosity.

- And to the Daughters of St. Paul for their encouragement and promotion of this work. The Sisters are a refreshing example of what happens when we "Do whatever he tells you."

The Purpose of This Book

Sometimes, having assented in mind and heart to the Gospel of Jesus Christ, people find themselves going through life as though on a roller coaster—with agonizingly slow climbs to the top, climbs filled with titillating dread of the certain rapid fall just beyond the high point.

There are many Christians who do not realize that Jesus does more than forgive. He has the power to deliver people from habitual sin. It is not arrogant or presumptuous to want to be holy and free from sin. It is not wrong to ask God to deliver us from this or that terrible temptation. In fact, that is precisely what God wants to give us—holiness, freedom from sin.

Do Whatever He Tells You is for people who want to experience victory over habitual sin, peace of mind in the midst of turmoil, freedom from overwhelming guilt, and joy in forgiveness and repentance. The "secret" to such a holy desire is to embrace God's will, to make it our own, to live with him, in him and for him.

"Pleasing God" is not the terrible chore it has been made out to be. It is not a gloomy way to live. In fact, you can only find joy when you please God.

Joy is that tremendous sense of elation in the presence of God. Joy is the fruit of a living faith that incorporates into your life the very power of Christ. It is that power which frees you from habitual sin, depression and discouragement. Such a faith is rooted in a pure and obedient heart. Only the pure and obedient heart can hope to rise above a culture that canonizes rebellion, promotes perversity and enslaves the weak and ignorant.

Mary, the Mother of Jesus, had such a heart. Her secret to joy and holiness is summed up in the last words she gives us in the Gospels of Jesus Christ. At the wedding feast in Cana, she told the servants, and she tells us today, "Do whatever he tells you" (see Jn. 2:5).

How to Use This Book

Do Whatever He Tells You is designed to serve as many people as possible—married and single; busy people with a tight schedule; people who have more time to read and to spend in personal reflection, examining their response to God at a more leisurely pace; people who want to spend time alone with God; people who want to spend time reflecting with spouses, prayer partners, parish discussion groups, fellow retreatants.

At the end of each chapter are two spiritual exercises—one for individuals, the other for two or more people who want to share their reflections and apply their insights to the larger community.

Each section is clearly marked: "For Individual Reflection" and "For Shared Reflection."

I recommend, for the most fruitful group reflection possible, that each member of the group do the individual reflections before sharing in group reflection.

Each personal reflection contains a scripture passage, a prayer, an examination of conscience, a decision and a closing prayer.

Each shared reflection contains a scripture passage, a prayer, and discussion questions which will help the group develop a community response to God's call, a decision, and a closing prayer.

In both private and group reflections, the "decisions" will provide readers with a concrete way to increase their response to the challenge, and their desire, to "Do whatever he tells you."

Chapter Two presents the Ten Commandments from the perspective of a loving Father who wants his children to achieve the maximum of their potential as human beings. At the end of Chapter Two is the first of the "examinations of conscience." In most cases, these examinations of conscience will be based on one or more of the Ten Commandments appropriate to the chapter.

At the end of Chapter Three, "Breaking the Cycle of Sin," I have included a list of "Things to Do," suggested spiritual activities to help people strengthen their resolve to avoid sin and pursue virtue.

It is advisable that each person doing the spiritual exercises (1) select a special time for prayer and reflection each day, (2) find a quiet place and (3) use a sacramental of some sort—a lighted candle, a crucifix, an icon, the Bible.

Each reflection contains a space for writing your "decisions" right in this book. However, you may prefer to use a private diary or journal to help record insights gained and decisions reached during each reflection. In shared reflections, there should be a "group journal" in which the main insights and decisions are recorded. The record of both individual and group reflections will help readers review their progress and growth.

You may want to use these reflections again in the future, so keep the book and your notes handy.

To get the most out of this book, each individual or group should spend a little quiet time before beginning each spiritual reflection and invite God to be with each of you and to fill you with an awareness of his presence. Spend a lot of time listening to God. Depending on your own needs, each personal reflection in this book could last from as little as fifteen minutes to as much as an hour.

God bless you in your prayer!

Chapter One

A Look at the Human Heart

"There are in the end three things that last: faith, hope and love, and the greatest of these is love" (1 Cor. 13:13).

I sat alone at a table next to a window in a second story hotel restaurant. Taxis were dropping off and picking up people on their way to and from the airport.

People milled around the entrance to the hotel. Others walked by on the street. There were families. There also were couples holding hands, walking leisurely down the street. I noticed one couple in particular. They seemed poor. The man leaned sideways, as though he suffered from a spinal defect, pushing his bicycle along with his right hand as he held a woman around the waist with his left. She was wearing a blue dress, far too tight for her bulk, and she looked even larger because the man was so thin.

Young people went by, walking, talking and laughing, holding hands, occasionally bumping one another in an intimate reminder of care and love.

Middle aged couples, as they strolled along, held hands, not tightly or possessively, just casually, with tender familiarity and reverence, each giving the other assurance, both sharing unspoken joy and love and sorrow, each touch rooted in a life of mutual giving.

Coupleness. Men and women are made to be together. They are made to love and be loved. The human heart yearns for love and is never at peace unless it is loving someone else.

Celibate people also have hearts that yearn to love—and they love, chastely, intimately, without conjugal expression of that love. They may love people of the opposite sex with a deep love, but their life is committed to a larger family, the family of the Church. They deny themselves husbands, wives and children so they can help the Church become a loving family.

The human heart must love or it dies. When a person is not loved and does not love, life becomes a depressing cycle of unfulfilled dreams, of hecticly, desperately grasped and discarded relationships. Sadly, people today have far too little chance to learn to love.

Love has to be learned. Love is not a feeling, not an emotion. Love is a conscious decision to live for the sake of another.

It is not good to talk about "the world" only in condemning terms. While St. Paul tells us in his letter to the Philippians that we are "in the midst of a twisted and depraved generation" (Phil. 2:15), that is only half the picture. Jesus himself reminds us that God loves the world: "Yes, God so loved the world that he gave his only Son, that whoever believes in him may not die but have eternal life. God did not send the Son into the world to condemn the world, but that the world might be saved through him" (Jn. 3:16-17).

Made in His Image

God made us in his image. That's why we love, need love and need to love. The second story of creation (see Gn. 2:4b-7; 18-25), if read with imagination, is a wonderful lesson in what it means to be human, to love and to be loved.

God created Adam. He formed him from clay. God breathed his very life into Adam. But Adam was alone. God wanted to make him some friends and playmates, other living creatures to keep him company. So God made the birds and the animals.

Notice how good God is. He made Adam from nothing. He didn't need Adam. God wasn't lonely. But he knew Adam would love to live—and he wanted to create a creature that would be more like him than any other visible creature. He gave Adam life.

Then, after he made the animals, he affirmed Adam's God-likeness. He gave him a share in creation. He said, "Adam, what in the world are we going to call all these animals?" With the intelligence God had given him, Adam named the giraffe, hippopotamus, dog, cat, lion, hummingbird, cow, horse and all the other creatures on land, in air and sea.

Adam looked on all these animals—but was still lonely.

And that was when God had that marvelous idea. He thought of Woman.

God caused Adam to go into a deep sleep. He took one of Adam's ribs and fashioned Eve. When Adam awoke, he didn't look at Eve calmly and say, "My, my God. What an intricate and complicated piece of creativity."

No. Adam was overwhelmed with joy. What he said amounted to, ''WOW! At last! Now you've really hit the jackpot, God! Here she is, the REST OF ME! Bone of my bone and flesh of my flesh!'' When Adam looked upon and loved Eve, he felt completeness! He experienced the fullness of what it means to be human. He was incomplete without Eve. Together, as couple, Adam and Eve reflected more completely the image of God because, ''God created man in his image; in the divine image he created him; male and female he created them'' (Gn. 1:27).

That's why men and women are so attracted to one another. Man is both male and female—and either is incomplete without the other. The attraction is much more than a sexual attraction. Sexual attraction is natural and it is sacred, coming from the creative and holy mind of God. But human sexuality is far more complex and wonderful than mere sexual intercourse.

People misunderstand human sexuality and human love. They use sex—or abuse it—in the name of love, even when there is no love at all. People talk about ''making love.'' You can't make love—and no amount of sexual activity will create intimacy and love if two people are uncommitted and just out for physical pleasure and mutual self-gratification.

There is more to the story of Genesis than the creation of the two sexes. God tells Adam and Eve, ''Be fertile and multiply; fill the earth and subdue it'' (Gn. 1:28). Genesis also tells us (2:24) that ''a man leaves his father and mother and clings to his wife, and the two of them become one body.''

In our ''twisted and perverse generation'' which ''God so loves'' there is a lot of coupling, but too little clinging, a lot of love talk, but too little love, a lot of mating, but a lot of distance from the responsibility of creating, protecting and sustaining new human life.

Sometimes, sexual activity, even in marriage, is totally divorced from the responsibility and God-given command to be fertile and fill the earth.

People who "make love" rather than learn to love usually end up rather miserable. Love is rooted in the heart and mind, not in the genitals.

So many teenagers are sexually active because they are seeking love. Many are scared and scarred by the divorce of their parents, many have been physically abused, many are confused by the troubles in the world and by their own blossoming minds and bodies. The clothing, cosmetic, automobile and entertainment industries have taken advantage of these young people— and of older people who have not yet matured. The industries provide as role models for happiness sleek and sexy-looking people. The commercials most often appeal to sexual instincts, pride, greed and lust for power and prominence.

It is hard for people, once they are trapped by the Great Lie, to believe in love.

But love is real.

Love Goes on No Matter What

One day a woman came to see me. She is the mother of a man serving a life sentence for murder. She spoke of her love for her son and her granddaughter. The granddaughter was deeply wounded by her father's crime and imprisonment. Her own mother rejected her. A trusted uncle molested her. She ran away from home, got hooked on drugs and had five babies out of wedlock, none of whom have the same father.

The elderly woman said, "I love them. Love isn't something you just turn off. Love goes on no matter what."

Love goes on no matter what—if it is really love, like God's love, like Adam's and Eve's love, like that woman's love for her son and granddaughter.

A young man fell in love. And he was loved in return. The young couple married. He came from a wealthy family. They "had everything going for them." Then tragedy struck. Just three months after their marriage, the young man suffered a terrible accident. As a result, he was paralyzed from the neck down. His wife found it very difficult to face the truth that, in the blush of their love, God would let something happen that would forever and drastically alter their lives.

She was tempted to leave him. He would have understood. But she stayed with him. And, as God would have it, she discovered that before the accident, she had conceived. Since the birth of their natural child, they have adopted other children.

Love, true love, goes on no matter what.

Happily the young man regained some use of his hands. His mind is crystal clear. He is self-employed. Their lives are rich and full.

The human heart, when it is true to itself, is true to God. The human heart is made in God's image, shares God's power to love, is fulfilled by loving and being loved.

In *Way, Truth and Life,* I said that God's laws and commandments are like the assembly and maintenance instructions we receive when we buy Christmas toys or appliances. God made us and he wants us to "work" right.

People resist the commandments of God because they do not know how much God loves them. They sometimes look upon God, along with "the Church," as alien and disembodied voices who have "never really lived." They misunderstand how present God is to us, how fully human Jesus was and how much he enjoyed the gift of human life.

God's commandments can be more meaningful—
and even welcome—when we realize how they help us
become more fully human, more fulfilled as persons.

Committed Christians obey God's commandments
for two reasons: God is God and deserves to be obeyed;
obeying God means a happier, healthier, holier life—
the kind of life he intended for his children before they
messed up their lives with sin.

After reflection, we will take a fresh look at those
commandments.

For Personal Reflection

Scripture
   "Then God said: 'Let us make man in our image, after our likeness. Let them have dominion over the fish of the sea, the birds of the air, and the cattle, and over all the wild animals and all the creatures that crawl on the ground.'

   "God created man in his image;
        in the divine image he created him;
        male and female he created them.

   "God blessed them, saying: 'Be fertile and multiply; fill the earth and subdue it'" (Gn. 1:26-28a).

Prayer
   Dear Lord, there are so many distractions. I am busy. So much demand is made on my time, money, skills. It is hard to concentrate on you, to be aware of your presence, to remember that you made me to be like you, to think your thoughts and love with your love. How can I train myself to be aware of your presence and to be totally dependent on you?

Examination of Conscience

• How can I become more aware of the goodness of God and remember that I am a wonderful creation, that he made me because he loves me?

• Do I encourage others to become all they were meant to become?

• Do I try to conserve natural resources and avoid waste of food, time, money?

• Am I consciously dependent on God? In what areas of my life do I most often—or least often—call on God for help and guidance?

Decision

Based on this reflection, I realize that to grow in my awareness of God as Creator and myself as part of his creation, I should _____

_____

_____

_____

_____

_____

_____ .

Prayer

Lord, I do love you and I want to love you more. Help me to stand before you with trust and love and admit all my faults while depending on your plentiful mercy for forgiveness and healing. Inspire me never to hide from you, for I cannot. You know me and love me as I am, and for this I am truly grateful. Help me to accept your forgiveness and my salvation as pure gifts from your completely selfless and divine love. Amen.

For Shared Reflection

Scripture

(Jesus said) "As the Father has loved me, so I have loved you. Live on in my love" (Jn. 15:9).

Prayer

Lord, the Church is strong when we together cooperate with your grace. We want to be a faithful Church whose love and joy reach out to bless and inspire others. Help us, Lord, always to remember that you made us, all of us, to be one.

Discussion Starters

1. Take a few minutes to share, if you so desire, insights from your private reflection.

2. Address these questions:

• In what ways can the secular community and other Christian churches look at our marriage, parish or prayer group and know that "love goes on no matter what?"

• Has our community witness been dampened by "business as usual" attitudes in our worship? Are we gratefully and faithfully dependent on God in all our ministries?

• Do we reflect God's love in our attitudes toward the sick, the poor, public sinners, prisoners, the disenfranchised, the lonely and otherwise needy? Are we a sign to the secular community that helping needy people is a top priority?

• What can we do, as a parish, to be a stronger witness for God in the secular community in which we live?

Decision

After reflecting on God's goodness and our response to his creative love, we realize we should _____

_____

_____

_____

_____ .

Prayer

Lord God, we praise you and thank you for your goodness, for life and for faith. Help us to become more aware of your presence in our lives. Help us to do what we have promised to do. Show us how to help others become more aware of you and learn to love you. Amen.

Chapter Two
Making Sense Out of Law

"Your heavenly Father knows all that you need" (Mt. 6:32b).

Many years ago, Cecile B. DeMille produced *The Ten Commandments*, a masterful movie which featured Charlton Heston as Moses. That movie is rerun on television almost every year during the Easter and Christmas seasons.

Mr. DeMille did a wonderful job in capturing the majesty of God, his power, his glory. Mr. Heston's Moses truly was inspirational. Scenes remain etched in the viewer's mind, even years after seeing the film.

Yet, was this movie as inspirational as it was entertaining? Did the medium become too much the message and the magic of cinema camouflage too well the mystery of a God who loves, who creates out of love, who comes to his people to teach them how to live?

Perhaps many people, when they think of God's commandments, imagine dark thunder clouds, flashing lightning and a fiery finger burning the commandments into stone while an overwhelmed Moses cowers before this unleashed and visible power of his transcendent God.

A Different Image of God

God is supreme. He has great glory, majesty and power—but he is also a gentle Father and he comes to us with great kindness. What would happen if people had a different image of God when they thought of his commandments? What would happen if, like the prophet Elijah, they saw God through new eyes?

Elijah was fleeing from a vengeful Jezebel who wanted him dead. He came to a cave and hid. God asked him why he was hiding. He told God it was because God's own people, the Israelites, had forsaken his Name. God told Elijah to go outside the cave for he would be passing by. You may want to read this account for yourself (see 1 Kgs. 19:1ff.).

When Elijah left the cave, a "strong and heavy wind was rending the mountains and crushing rocks before the LORD—but the LORD was not in the wind. After the wind, there was an earthquake—but the LORD was not in the earthquake. After the earthquake was a fire—but the LORD was not in the fire. After the fire there was a tiny whispering sound. When he heard this, Elijah hid his face in his cloak and went and stood at the entrance of the cave."

Think of God in this way, as a Father who comes whispering gently into your ear. He loves you, embraces you and wants you to experience his gentle and compassionate love, his wisdom and understanding. He wants you to know what it means to be his own daughter or son, to experience fully and consciously the truth that he made you in his image, to be his heir, to be with him for all eternity.

When our eldest grandchild was just a tiny baby, he became very ill. He couldn't keep down any food. I remembered an old home remedy—a soft-boiled fresh egg with saltine crackers crumbled finely into the egg. I gave that to the baby and he kept it down.

But I did more. I bundled him up, for it was a cool autumn day at Fort Stewart, GA, and I took him for a walk. He was only two months old and surely he could not understand anything I said to him. Yet, I had to talk to him and let him know he was not alone, that he was loved.

"Kenny," I said, "we love you. You belong to us, with us. We want you to live. Always remember that you're a Catholic."

Why was it so important for me to talk to an infant who could not understand? Somehow, in my heart, I knew he would sense my love. I had a personal need to let him know we were his family and we loved him and wanted to care for him.

Is it so hard to imagine God like that?

A New Look at the Ten Commandments

Let's look at the Ten Commandments (see Dt. 5:6ff.) through this model of the gentle, loving Father wanting nothing but the best for his child. Perhaps, in this way, we will find greater motivation and the means to overcome temptations and weaknesses and to resist sin.

"I am the Lord.... You shall not have other gods besides me."

Imagine God holding you in his arms, understanding how ignorant and helpless you are compared with him, telling you, "Dear child, I made you. I am your God. I want you to inherit everything I have. I want you to live fully—that's why I have breathed my very life into you. My life is a life of goodness, integrity, holiness, power.

"If you want to live my life, if you want to know personally what it means to be a human made in my image, if you want to live forever with me, then just remember, I am the Lord, your God. You must not have strange gods in my place. If you walk away from me, you walk away from the source of your life, you walk away from peace, from life everlasting. It's not that I'm so picky. I'm not proud, my child, but I am Life and I am Love. Leave me and you embrace both hatred and death."

Isn't that a more appealing image than a distant, thundering, lightning-wielding God throwing down ultimatum after ultimatum from heaven?

And let's go on.

———————

"You shall not take the name of the Lord, your God, in vain."

There is hardly a popular movie today which does not blaspheme the Lord. The names, Christ and Jesus, are used as common slang. Sometimes, the name of our blessed Savior is coupled with some of the sleaziest and most wicked scenes imaginable.

God is deeply offended and hurt by this—and so are all those who love him. Think. How much do you revere your own name? Would you like for someone to use your name to promote evil? It would be terribly unjust for someone to claim you are sponsoring an orgy or selling crack when you are not.

But too many people abuse God's name this way, tying his name to all sorts of trivia or evil.

I can imagine the Lord saying, "My child, my name does not mean evil. It means love, healing, forgiveness. Why do you use my name to curse others? What makes my name so handy and profane in your eyes? I love everyone. I don't want anyone damned—and if they are damned it is their fault and not mine. Don't ask me to damn your enemies. I want to save both you and your enemies. I want you to become brothers and sisters. And don't treat my name as a handy slang word that helps you vent off steam or show off."

God is all good, all holy and almighty. He deserves our total respect and reverence. No one who knows God and loves him would even try to justify using his name thoughtlessly or maliciously.

I wonder how many people, with so much blasphemy all around us, really understand the seriousness of this sin.

And God says...

"Take care to keep holy the Sabbath day."

Today people have compromised so much that Sunday is truly just like any other day: shopping malls are open and going great guns, as are night clubs and so-called adult entertainment centers.

In his goodness and wisdom, God tells us that we need to stop our frantic labors one day a week to reflect on life and on our relationship with him, to give our minds, spirits and bodies much needed rest, to renew and strengthen family relationships and friendships, to take time out for deeper and more rewarding prayer.

Because we have pictured God as this demanding ego-maniac who doesn't understand how important it is for us to work that extra day, or go shopping or "have a blast," we miss the wonderful guidance God is giving us.

In the commandment to observe the Sabbath, God is saying, "My children, you simply can't continue to function, to live peaceful and fruitful lives if you are constantly running. You keep on running like this and you'll be burnt out physically, mentally and spiritually. You will become estranged from your family and from me."

What is it that drives us so? Not God. Not the quest for inner peace, for personal strength and holiness. We are running away from something. Maybe we are running away from ourselves. Maybe we are afraid to stop and do nothing because we will have to think about our lives and how we are abusing the gifts of time, talent and treasure.

As long as we are running, we don't have to think. We can fool ourselves into thinking we are really doing well. "After all," thinks the hard-working parent, "I am putting in 60 hours a week for the sake of my children." Or the social worker can say, "I am actually working for God all day long, seven days a week, so my entire life is a prayer."

One's life is supposed to be a prayer—but prayer is in large part listening to God. If a person is too busy to take time out to pray, too busy to obey God's command to keep holy that one day a week, then it is very difficult to believe that one's life will indeed be a prayer.

There's danger in working for God. We can do all manner of things we want to do and offer it all to God. The real challenge is to do God's work, to do what God wants.

He gave us the Sabbath for our own good. The Sabbath can help us stop running and truly start living.

"Honor your father and your mother."

This is the only one of the Ten Commandments to which God has attached a specific, promised reward. The one who honors his father and mother will "have a long life and prosperity in the land which the Lord, your God, is giving you."

Now, not everyone who has honored his or her parents has lived a long life. We have to see this commandment within the context of all of salvation history and realize that the best kind of "long life" is eternal life!

What makes this commandment so special? Why is God urging us to honor our parents?

In the first place, "honor" here seems to mean much more than mere respect, obedience, being nice and doing all the chores assigned by one's parents.

We all enter into a fundamental relationship with our parents, and through them we learn to relate with our siblings, with other people, with God and with life itself.

Life is a universal reality. It is more than the collection of all individual lives. Life is an extension of the Creator himself—and all creatures that live or have lived are somehow related and, drawn together, share the same fountain, the same God, the same Father.

St. Francis must have had a tremendous appreciation for life and the relationship of all living things. His awe extended even to inanimate objects, such as his "Brother Sun" and "Sister Moon."

When God tells us to honor our parents, he is telling his children, "You didn't just accidentally come upon this earth. No, I truly planned you. When I created Adam and Eve, I was already thinking about you. I knew you would be born of the parents I gave you. Why did I make you? Because I knew you would love to live , I wanted you to know my love for you, and I want you to love me, too.

"Your parents are a sign of my creative power; they are the channel of grace through which I chose to give you life. To dishonor your parents is a direct insult to me, a rejection of the unbroken chain of human life all the way back to the Garden of Eden. If you dishonor your parents, you dishonor life itself and you dishonor me, the source and end of all life."

"You shall not kill."

God is the source of life, the creator of life, the master of life. Only God has the right to end life.

Murder is a terrible crime. It takes another's life. Murder cannot destroy eternal life, but to kill a human being is to interfere with the normal process of life, to remove that person from a family, from dependent children, from society, from friends and associates.

To kill someone is to play God, to make oneself the lord of one particular life.

As we have seen from the commandment to honor parents, to sin against one life is to sin against and threaten all life and to sin against God.

If we can imagine God as a gentle and loving Father, what is he trying to tell us when he says, "You shall not kill"?

Could he be trying to tell us that he has no favorites; that each and every living human being is gifted with life with all of his love; that prince is not loved more than pauper; that police officer and killer are loved equally; that the unborn is as beloved as the gurgling toddler; that the comatose patient is as fully alive in God's eyes as is the football player making a touchdown in the Super Bowl?

Is God telling us in this commandment that anger and vicious words are a sin against life itself? Hatred and vicious anger pave the way to murder—and even if murder never occurs, to hate and be verbally or physically abusive are sins against human life and dignity. No one has the right to hate or abuse another.

God loves each of us equally, with the fullness of his love, his power. He cannot love by degrees. He loves each of us as much as he loves Jesus. He gives each of us *all his love simultaneously!*

We cannot understand that kind of love—but that is no reason not to believe in it.

Whether we are saints or sinners, young or old, rich or poor, ugly or pretty, God's love goes on no matter what.

Because God loves us, he cares about how we treat our own bodies. Smoking, overeating, drinking to excess—all these are actions which endanger life and therefore are against life. A pro-life worker puffing on a cigarette, a Christian overdrinking, overeating or driving recklessly are counter signs to our proclaimed faith and respect for life.

"You shall not commit adultery."

I've already mentioned sexual immorality. However, I think it is important to consider two points in seeing this commandment through new eyes.

First, there are very practical reasons for this commandment, reasons born of love for the human family and God's holy desire that his family will be one in love.

Adultery is infidelity. It is no surprise that throughout the Old Testament God speaks of his people as "adulterous" when they forsake him for false gods.

In God's eyes, sexual relations are part and parcel of the covenant between a man and woman to love one another, to forsake all others, to be "fertile and subdue the earth." Sexual relations are both a sign of unity between husband and wife and a means of strengthening their love. Sexual relations are also the means God chose to procreate new life.

If husband and wife are not faithful to one another, especially to the point that adultery results, the entire foundation for wholesome family life is destroyed. The adulterer or adulteress takes what belongs to the spouse and gives it to another. In marriage we give ourselves to one another. That means that a spouse has exclusive rights—in union with God's will—over the heart, mind and body of his wife or her husband. Married people cannot simply live for themselves. They have taken vows to live for their partners, to be faithful and to love no matter what.

Sound familiar? Sure, it does. This is the kind of faithfulness promised at every Christian wedding.

This notion of marital fidelity is familiar for another reason, which brings me to the second point I would like to make: the covenant between husband and wife is rooted in and echoes the covenant between God and his people. God promised the Hebrew people that he would be their God. He promised he would never stop loving them and gave them chance after chance to come back after being unfaithful.

Pope John Paul II has said that the marital covenant gives flesh in time and space, in our very lives, to the covenant of God with his people. The sacrament of marital love is a sign of God's covenant with his people, and of Christ's with his Church.

Unfaithful spouses make a lie of God's covenant— and no one, not even liars, can believe a lie. Adultery weakens the witness God wants present in marital love —and since that witness is weakened, we are all poorer and have more trouble believing in God's own faithfulness to us.

———

"You shall not steal."

We all know it is wrong to steal. Stealing, for most of us, is an overt act: taking someone's money from a school locker, stealing a car or taking someone's stereo. But stealing can be far more subtle.

One of the greatest signs of social decay is the lack of honesty in our culture—and the growing acceptance of falsehood as part and parcel of everyday business and personal relationships.

An automobile dealer advertises a brand new truck for only $6,600. An eager customer may drive miles to discover that this price does not include "dealer prep" ($600), administrative costs ($100), shipping costs ($500), a rear bumper ($200)—and other costs. The final and true price is closer to $9,000.

This is false advertising at best, but it borders on stealing. Some people, young and old, can be dazzled by the shine of a new car or truck, beguiled by the subtle but clear implication that social acceptance, prestige and happiness come with the vehicle, and fooled into believing they have really struck a bargain.

We all know that it is wrong to take what belongs to someone else—either by force or trickery.

There are exceptions when stealing is not a sin—such as being forced to steal at gunpoint, or stealing food when that's the only way you can keep your family from starving.

Exceptions aside, stealing shows utter contempt for the life and rights of the victim. Stealing says, "You are nothing and nobody and your rights and feelings are totally beside the point. I want what you have, and I will take what you have because I want what I want."

In his love, God has told us this is wrong. But, if you look at all of creation through God's eyes, if you admit that he loves everyone equally, can "stealing" take on a larger meaning than simply *taking something away* from someone? Could stealing not also mean *keeping something away* from someone?

Pope Paul VI, in his encyclical *On the Development of Peoples*, said that people with surplus wealth have what truly belongs to the poor. In other words, it is not only charitable to give from our abundance, it is essentially a matter of justice. Justice because God provides the world's goods and power for the benefit of all.

God does not will that some people and nations horde their wealth while others starve, that some people have 10 (or 200) pairs of shoes while others have none. God has provided adequately for all the people he has placed on earth. People, not God, have upset the balance of wealth and power that God intended should be maintained through the virtues of love and justice.

Is the Father not whispering quietly into our ears, in the present day, that the empty rooms in our homes should be used for the homeless, that the extra money in the bank should be used to help the poor, that the extra food in the pantry rightfully belongs to those who have no food?

If we Christians really want to respond to God's love, we must listen carefully to what he says and rise to the challenge to do whatever he tells us. There is no doubt that he is urging everyone to share their resources and gifts with others.

Selfishness is one of the greatest sins in America—along with sexual immorality. Both sins are closely linked because they are born of pride and lust.

"You shall not bear false witness against your neighbor."

This commandment means a lot more than not lying to Judge Wapner, hero of television's popular "People's Court."

This commandment tells us not to lie about one another, not to gossip, for a person's good name means the world to him or her. As we must not take God's name in vain, so we must not abuse the good name of our brother and sister.

Lying has almost become a national pastime. It's cute to lie—and so convenient.

Truth sometimes hurts, but in the end, truth sets us free. As a young boy in Louisiana, I joined some friends in stealing watermelons from a farmer. Now that is really not a terribly serious sin, but because the farmer was black, we thought it would be funny to run our horses through his entire melon patch—and we did, destroying many of the melons and the vines as well.

For days, I moped about, with my face dragging around my ankles. I felt awful, sort of dirty. I felt I had not lived up to what my parents had taught me about being kind and considerate to everyone—and I hadn't.

One day, Mama said, "Junior, if something's on your mind that you need to get off it, you'd better tell me. Remember that if you tell the truth I will never punish you." So I told her what we had done. She admonished me, and sent me off to confession. As I look back, I remember the sudden relief I felt as I told the truth. For my forming conscience, keeping silent about the sin was as bad as lying, so convinced was I—and still am—that total honesty means admitting what I have done wrong, regardless of the consequences.

But, concerning that event many years ago, there is still a nagging corner of my conscience that is not satisfied. Mama never made me go tell that black farmer that I was sorry. He 's dead now, and I can't tell him. And that makes me even sadder about it all.

Truth indeed sets us free.

Lies destroy.

Back in seventh grade, a very poor girl was the object of much ridicule. Some of the boys in the class started a vicious rumor about the girl and, it seemed to her, that everybody was laughing at her and talking about her.

She was crushed.

Finally someone told her what was being said—and, further, told her he didn't believe the lie. The girl was deeply touched by this act of friendship, and since she then knew what the rumor was all about, she was able to put an end to it.

When we hurt people, we say they are unimportant objects just to be used for our own sick pleasures. When we treat people like that, we are hurting God, for Jesus said that whatever we do to others we do to him (see Mt. 25:31ff.).

"You shall not covet your neighbor's wife."

In the old days, men owned their wives, to be bought and sold, to be used or abused. The commandment could have been interpreted to mean basically, don't envy your neighbor's possessions. But, God, knowing that women are equal (if not more than equal!) to men, had something else in mind. It seems that coveting another man's wife is courting thoughts of adultery as well as threatening the sanctity and peace of a marriage and family. Paying too much attention to someone else's wife or husband will at least put a strain on that marriage if it does not create jealousy and mistrust.

In his kindness, God is telling us, "Keep your thoughts pure and honorable so your actions can be pure and honorable and peace may reign in all of your hearts and homes."

"You shall not covet your neighbor's goods."

Again, don't even desire what others have. That's envy. Envy and greed go hand-in-hand and lead to all sorts of abuse, including injustice, calumny, slander, stealing and all kinds of violence. The saints of the Church have told us that one way to overcome envy and jealousy is to praise God for his kindness to others. If you're thanking God for the Kennedy family's wealth, it will be hard for you to envy them.

Toward Conversion of Heart

God comes to each of us, anew. He is not bound up in the pages of the Bible or locked away in the tabernacles of our churches. He is a gentle God, a loving God, even though he is truly a powerful God and a just God.

If you have had trouble believing that God is really concerned with your life and holiness, try to do what Elijah did. Be silent in the sanctuary of your heart and listen for him in the quiet sound of your conscience. He will speak to you of love and give you the wisdom to embrace his way to peace and a good life.

Mary, the mother of Jesus, must have had a perfectly ordered life. Her life must really have been a prayer of praise to the Father.

She could face the challenge to be the unwed Mother of God's only begotten Son. She could face the loneliness when Joseph died and Jesus left her for his public ministry. She could face the ridicule of the disbelievers—and, yes, she could face the sight of her Son, the Son of God, dying on the cross.

Mary had no strange gods standing between her and God. She did not worship money or power.

She kept holy his name. So perfect was her love and worship of God that the Angel Gabriel could say to her, "Hail! Full of grace! The Lord is with you!"

Mary kept the Sabbath along with her parents and all the other faithful Jews. She used that holy day to draw deeper into the heart and mind of God. Her openness to God's love and his will made her ready to tackle the greatest ministry of any woman on earth—bringing Jesus into the world, nurturing him, training him, and yes, even teaching him, the Son of God, to pray.

Mary honored her parents. She lived with them. And she honored all the elders in her family. She left shortly after conceiving of the Holy Spirit, to assist her aged cousin, Elizabeth, who was to give birth to John the Baptizer.

Mary remained a virgin all her life, according to the teachings and tradition of the Church. She never had relations with Joseph and therefore never had other children. Mary was pure. This does not mean that she was pure because she did not have sexual relations with her husband. There is nothing impure about conjugal love in a marriage. Mary's purity is born of her total obedience to God. If God had wanted her to have other children with her husband, she would have. Whatever she knew God wanted of her, she complied.

It would be hard to imagine Mary stealing, lying about a neighbor or breaking any of the other commandments.

Yet, we must always remember that Mary was totally human. Her holiness came from God, just as ours must if we are ever to be holy.

Like Mary, you must remember that, because God loves you, you should desire to do whatever he tells you to do.

If you want to find pure joy, know that it is found only in pleasing God. Not because God gives you goodies when you are good, but because pure joy is possible only when we are one with God. He made us in his image, to be with him, in him, of him. There is only one way to please God—and that is to enter into intimate communion with him. When we let God take us into himself, we find our true selves—and in finding our true selves, in the heart of God, so to speak, we find peace and joy.

Entering into a deep and intimate relationship with God means to experience conversion, to accept his Word, Jesus, as the ultimate truth. It means to turn away (repent) from our former responses and reactions to temptation, challenges and disappointments and to

embrace Jesus' Way. And finally, it means that we become his disciples, we follow Jesus without reservation, we become as committed as he to the Father's will
and kingdom. We live as brothers and sisters of Jesus,
sons and daughters of God.

If you have not already decided to follow Jesus, I
urge you to make that commitment right now. It's simple. All you have to do is say:

*"Jesus, I want you to be the Lord of my life. I'm
sorry for all my sins. Please forgive me and make me
your own."*

Then, after making this personal commitment, find
a priest, seek baptism or reconciliation and get back
into the mainstream of the sacramental life of the
Church.

Remember, accepting Jesus as Lord does not put an
end to spiritual struggle. All Christians must carry
their cross, part of which means remaining faithful
during even the most difficult temptations.

Once you accept Jesus, you may find that you're on
that roller coaster, going up and down, having too
many high points from which you fall into thought or
behavior you know is not right. Maybe you feel like
groaning with St. Paul, "I cannot even understand my
own actions. I do not do what I want to do but what I
hate" (Rom. 7:15).

We can be sure of two things: (1) No matter how
holy we become we will always find ways to sin, and
(2) no matter how sinful we are, God's mercy is always
there for the asking.

No need, really, to convince ourselves we are
sinners—but we may need to consider the wonderful
truth about God's mercy. God's mercy not only forgives
sin, but delivers us from sin.

We have all heard that we must pray to be able to
resist temptation—and so we must. But, not everyone

has been told that we can pray for deliverance from habitual sin and truly expect to be delivered.

We'll talk about deliverance in the next chapter.

For Personal Reflection

Scripture

"Hear, O Israel! The LORD *is our God, the* LORD *alone! Therefore, you shall love the* LORD, *your God, with all your heart, and with all your soul, and with all your strength. Take to heart these words which I enjoin on you today. Drill them into your children. Speak of them at home and abroad, whether you are busy or at rest"* (Dt. 6:4-7).

Prayer

Dear Lord, I have to admit that sometimes you seem far away, a strange and alien God. In those times, I find it hard to believe that you care for me and live in me. Maybe, Lord, I am afraid to feel your presence in my life because I would have to face the challenge of change.

With gentleness and compassion, Father, let me see myself through your eyes as I meditate on your commandments. Don't let me hide my sins. Let me face them squarely. But, don't let me despair because I have sinned. I pray that your Holy Spirit may enlighten me. In what ways, O Lord, have I offended you?

Examination of Conscience

I, the Lord, am your God... You shall not have other gods besides me.

- Do I see myself as a child of God—or is that simply too good to be true?

- Have I at times put my trust in worldly power—in money and prestige, in popularity and personal gifts?

- Do I place my trust and hope in "Lady Luck," dreaming of that big break, such as winning the lottery? Or do I give mere creatures credit for powers that only God has—such as the stars and rabbits' feet and fortune tellers?

- Do I run away from truth, responsibility, the past or the future by relying on alcohol, drugs or other false securities?

You shall not take the Name of the Lord, your God, in vain.

- Do I curse, swear unnecessarily, use God's name as slang?

- Do I realize that to name God is to ask him to witness whatever I am doing at the moment? Do I ask God to witness evil?

- Am I sometimes so angry that I ask God to curse my enemies, or even my brothers and sisters, all of whom he loves as much as he loves me?

Take care to keep holy the sabbath day.

- Do I respect the Lord's Day? Are my Sundays set aside for church, prayer, family time and reflection on my life and relationship with God?

- Do I shop on Sundays, encouraging businesses to stay open and deprive their employees of spending the Lord's Day with their families?

- In my play on Sundays, do I use my mind, body, gifts and money in ways that help others and honor God?

Decision

To root out of my life any semblance of idolatry and any disrespect for the Lord's name and the Sabbath, I will

_____

_____

_____

_____

_____ .

Prayer

I believe in you, almighty, holy and Triune God. You are Father, Son and Spirit. I renounce all false gods in my life. I acclaim you as my only God. I pledge, by your grace, to honor you, to bless your name and to keep every Sunday as a day in which I spend special time in prayer, renewing my relationship with you, my family and friends. May you be praised forever. Amen.

For Shared Reflection

Scripture

"I will give you a new heart and place a new spirit within you, taking from your bodies your stony hearts and giving you natural hearts. I will put my spirit within you and make you live by my statutes, careful to observe my decrees. You shall live in the land I gave your fathers; you shall be my people, and I will be your God" (Ez. 36:26-28).

Prayer

Lord, you call us as a people. There is no such thing as a Lone Ranger Christian. We are all one in you. As a community of believers, we want our lives to proclaim that you are One, Holy and Almighty, that we honor your name and that we worship you in purity of heart and with all our mind and strength. Help us, Lord, to be your people, a faithful people who will give you both joy and honor.

Discussion Starters

There are a lot of tensions in the Church today. Catholics, and indeed all Christians, must remain faithful to God in all things. Part of being faithful to God is to love as he loves—in all things.

Please reflect on the following:

- Some people compare today's American culture with that of ancient Rome, in which there were many false gods. Are there indeed false gods in our lives today? If so, what or who are they? How did they become "gods"?

- Sometimes, people use religion merely as a security blanket and never permit themselves to go deeper than superficial piety. Is this a form of idolatry? If so, how does it develop and how can it be overcome?

- In what ways might our family, parish or diocese help restore respect for the Sabbath?

- How can we promote respect for God's name in our parish and secular community? Would it help to revitalize such organizations as the Holy Name Society?

Decision

To become a more effective force in helping ourselves and others honor God and make him the center of our lives, we have decided to_____

_____

_____

_____

_____

_____

_____ .

Prayer

Jesus, please help us to know God intimately and experience him as a kind and loving, though just, Father. Through your passion, death and resurrection, obtain for us the grace of true worship, faithfulness to truth, love for the Name and Word of God, and the wisdom to help restore the world to the kingdom of God. Amen.

Chapter Three

Breaking the Cycle of Sin

"Before faith came, we were under the constraint of the law, locked in until the faith that was coming should be revealed. In other words, the law was our monitor until Christ came to bring about our justification through faith" (Gal. 3:23-24).

As important as the commandments were to Saint Paul, who was a Jew, he saw them as rules and regulations which, apart from Christ, had little or no meaning.

"The law" was not simply the Ten Commandments. It was the whole of Hebraic religious law—more than 600 rules by which the faithful Jew was to live.

These laws were rooted in revelation, were at least indirectly given the Chosen People by God. In Paul's eyes, however, they were useless and powerless compared with the person of Jesus Christ.

The laws were good—and our own Code of Canon Law in the Catholic Church is good. But when law becomes an end in itself, when people begin measuring their own worth, importance and piety by law rather than by relationship, the law becomes a burden to faith rather than an aid to holiness.

This, it seems, is what Paul fought against. "The law" was in place and God's people were "locked" under its constraint. The law, of itself, had no power to redeem, to forgive, to heal, to bless. The law, without a relationship with God, stood outside the human heart, became an external code and did not foster internal conversion.

Paul knew and tells us that Jesus, unlike the law, is God incarnate. He has of himself the divine nature, the power to teach, heal, bless and forgive. His death atones for all sin. His resurrection credibly promises eternal life.

Paul chooses Jesus over the law. Jesus is the Way, the Truth and the Life (see Jn. 14:6) and in him alone is salvation. A deep, intimate relationship with Jesus as Lord, Savior and brother gives the believer a share in the very life of Jesus, in his gifts and power. In him, we become sons and daughters of God. Faith, to Paul and all the other saints both here and in heaven, is nothing less than intimate communion with God. Through faith, we become immersed in God's goodness, his holiness. We are elevated above the natural and given a share in divinity.

The law cannot do this. The Ten Commandments cannot do this. Novenas cannot do this. Nothing can do this apart from faith in the Lord Jesus.

When we have faith in God, then his commandments make sense. They become part of our own values, because we see more clearly that his commandments come from his great wisdom as well as from his love for us. He knows what is best for us.

The Key to Defeating Sin

Here lies the key to breaking bad habits, habitual sin, improper and unhealthy attitudes. We cannot look at sin as digression from the law—but as separation from Jesus, who has won victory over sin—and more, who is himself victory over sin!

A very dear friend, Father Michael, who works with Mother Angelica at the Eternal Word Television Network in Birmingham, had a wonderful insight into the power of Christ to overcome sin. The key to growth in holiness, he said, is to admit that we are powerless to save ourselves, powerless even to overcome those sins which plague us so much.

Father Michael points to Paul's letter to the Romans and what Paul has to say about being dead to sin. Actually, it is most helpful to reflect on that entire section of Romans (6:1-14), but here I will quote only from verse 6:

"This we know: our old self was crucified with him so that the sinful body might be destroyed and we might be slaves to sin no longer."

What does it mean to be dead to sin but alive to Christ? If a drug addict is dead, heroin injected into his body will not affect him in any way. He is dead and his body will not respond to the drug.

When we were baptized, we died with Christ—and we rose with him. He is dead to sin and alive for God. We, who are now one with him, are also dead to sin. We should be, in a sense, immune to sin.

"But," someone objects, "we still sin." Yes, we do. However, the enticements of Satan and the world should not enslave the person born again in Jesus Christ. No Christian, truly in love with and a slave to Jesus Christ, will ever be in bondage to sin.

Baptism is not some magical trick that takes us out of the world and sets us up in some sort of heaven on

earth. St. Paul himself said, that because of the extra-
ordinary revelations he had received from God, God
gave him "a thorn in the flesh, an angel of Satan to beat
me and keep me from getting proud. Three times I
begged the Lord that this might leave me. He said to
me, 'My grace is enough for you, for in weakness power
reaches perfection.' And so I willingly boast of my
weaknesses instead, that the power of Christ may rest
upon me" (2 Cor. 12:7-9).

That same saint said, "I have been crucified with
Christ, and the life I live now is not my own; Christ is
living in me. I am still living my human life, but it is
a life of faith in the Son of God, who loved me and gave
himself for me" (Gal. 2:19b-20).

It's hard to understand. Even St. Paul (or our
translators) find it difficult to explain how we are no
longer "living our own life" but a "life of faith" and
still "living our own human life."

The Power of Faith

The key word, of course, is faith. Faith makes
changes in us. We are transformed, through faith, into
the image of God. Faith does not take away our person-
alities or our free will. Faith is a great gift from God that
(1) enables us to believe in him, (2) gives us a share in
his life and (3) makes us children of God.

It is through faith—living with, in and for Jesus—
that we can change our behavior and thinking patterns.

It is Jesus who conquers sin, not we. That's what
St. Paul means when he tells us through Romans to be
dead to sin. It is through our flight to Jesus in time of
temptation (our boast that we are weak) that we find the
victory over temptation and sin.

For Catholics, the Eucharist is the real presence of
Jesus. At Mass we stand at the foot of the Cross and

look upon our crucified Lord. We stand at the empty tomb and know that he is risen.

At the Mass, as the host and cup are elevated, call upon Jesus to take away those terrible temptations which make life miserable. Try this, if you want a wonderful surprise. Just look up at the elevated host and cup and say, "Jesus, you know I love you. I can't overcome my great problem. Only you can do it. Please Jesus, I give myself to you. Please deliver me from (name the temptation or sin)."

As you sit in your pew after Communion, repeat the prayer—and then thank Jesus for what he is doing in your life.

Jesus has already defeated sin. We need only to flee to his protection, enter more deeply into his love and be more open to his power.

Sure, we will sin again—but there is a difference in committing sins occasionally and being overwhelmed by sin or being "in bondage" to sin.

The prayer to our Eucharistic Jesus will help us break the hellish cycle of sin, and more—it will help us to bounce back quickly when we do sin and to seek his loving mercy right away.

Once a young man complained to a saintly priest about "constantly falling flat on my face."

"My son," said the priest, "when you fall flat on your face, you are still pointed in the same direction. Raise your eyes and you will see the hand of Jesus ready to lift you up."

It is important, however, not to slough off sin. We can never break the bonds of habitual sin if we do not confess and repent.

St. Augustine, a great saint who was first a great sinner, said:

"Let us never assume that if we live good lives we will be without sin; our lives should be praised only when we continue to beg for pardon. But men are

hopeless creatures, and the less they concentrate on their own sins, the more interested they become in the sins of others. They seek to criticize, not to correct. Unable to excuse themselves, they are ready to accuse others. This was not the way David showed us how to pray to make amends to God when he said, 'I acknowledge my transgressions, and my sin is ever before me.' He did not concentrate on others' sins; he turned his thoughts on himself. He did not merely stroke the surface, but he plunged inside and went deep down within himself. He did not spare himself, and therefore was not impudent in asking to be spared...

"We should be displeased with ourselves when we commit sin, for sin is displeasing to God. Sinful though we are, let us at least be like God in this, that we are displeased at what displeases him. In some measure then you will be in harmony with God's will, because you find displeasing in yourself what is abhorrent to your Creator." (A sermon of St. Augustine from the Liturgy of the Hours, Book III, Page 450-1, Catholic Book Publishing, 1975.)

Now seems to be a good time to pause for reflection and prayer.

For Personal Reflection

Scripture

(The father of a boy possessed by an evil spirit approached Jesus.) " 'If out of the kindness of your heart you can do anything to help us, please do!' Jesus said, " 'If you can?" Everything is possible to a man who trusts.' The boy's father immediately exclaimed, 'I do believe! Help my lack of trust!'" (Mk. 9:14-29)

Prayer

Lord, I believe but I, too, often lack trust. Sometimes, Jesus, I'm afraid to ask for holiness. The very thought of changing my life scares me. As miserable as I am, I at least know what I'm facing. Holiness, a future without my present habits, scares me or seems beyond reach. But right now, Lord, I ask for the special grace to always pray as you did in the Garden of Gethsemane: "Not my will, but yours be done."

Mary, Mother of God and my Mother, please intercede for me before Jesus and the Father. Pray, Mary, that I may be truly sorry for all my sins and faithful to the call of Jesus to trust in him and in him alone. Mary, you are holy and know the heart of God. Pray for me that I, too, may be holy and live in a way totally pleasing to God. Amen.

Examination of Conscience

You shall not commit adultery.

You shall not covet your neighbor's wife.

Human love is supposed to be a sign of God's love for his people. The world speaks of love but means self-gratification and lust. Many popular "love songs" pass selfishness off as love. Am I converting the world or is the world converting me?

- In my relationships, do I respect others as persons who are precious, lovable and dignified in the eyes of God?

- Do selfishness and lust find expression in my life as sexual sins, committed alone or with others?

- Overeating is also a "sin of the flesh." Do I live to eat rather than eat to live?

- Do I endanger marital relationships by an unhealthy desire for another's spouse? Do I engage in flirtations that can cause division and distrust?

- Do I monitor TV programs and reading material in my own home?

Decision

(Remember, you may use the space provided here, or a private notebook, or both, to record your decisions.)

To respond positively to the insights the Lord has given me in this reflection, I shall, in faith _____

_____

_____

_____

_____

_____

_____

_____ .

Prayer

My sins and weaknesses cause deep shame in my life, Lord. My feelings, attitudes and actions often fall short of what you expect of me. I know you can deliver me from habitual sin and strengthen me in temptation. Please do so—and I will tell everyone of your great goodness and encourage others to put their trust in you. Amen.

Things to Do

If you need to strengthen your faith and resolve to let Jesus help you defeat sin in your life, any of the following "things to do" may be helpful.

- The next time I go to Mass, I will look upon my Eucharistic Lord and ask him, by the power of his passion, death and resurrection, to deliver me from bondage to sin and to help me live in the joy of holiness.

- If I have not been taking advantage of the Sacrament of Reconciliation (confession), I will begin again to use this means of reconciliation, at least on a monthly basis.

- I will daily, for one week, reflect on Romans 6:1ff., asking Jesus to help me understand the miracle of being dead to sin and alive in him.

- Every Friday, I will pray the Sorrowful Mysteries of the Rosary, contemplating the price of my salvation.

- I will try to help a depressed person find hope in Jesus through my own love, friendship and faith.

- I will share some of the fruit of my daily reflections and prayer with my spouse, family, prayer partner or parish small group.

For Shared Reflection

Scripture

"I charge you to preach the word, to stay with this task whether convenient or inconvenient—correcting, reproving, appealing—constantly teaching and never losing patience. For the time will come when people will not tolerate sound doctrine, but, following their own desires, will surround themselves with teachers who tickle their ears. They will stop listening to the truth and will wander off to fables. As for you, be steady and self-possessed; put up with hardship, perform your work as an evangelist, fulfill your ministry" (2 Tm. 4:2-5).

Prayer

Lord Jesus, you gave us apostles, prophets and teachers. You promised to keep our Church from error. You call each of us to stand for truth, to explain truth to others.

Sometimes, Jesus, we hear different opinions about truth—and even when truth is clear, it is hard to live truth.

Please help us to embrace your Word with total love and commitment, as individuals and as a believing community. Amen.

Discussion Starters

If our community of faith is to help people break the cycle of sin and to recognize and embrace truth, we must review with open minds and hearts the teachings of the Church's magisterium and the dissent from that teaching.

With a view toward reconciliation of differences and development of a stronger commitment to truth, reflect together on the following issues:

- Some people no longer consider pre-marital sex a sin. Still, the Church teaches that sexual intercourse is permissible only in marriage. What lies at the foundation of the Church's teaching?

- Some people claim that homosexual activity, masturbation and artificial birth control, in spite of the magisterium's position, are permissible. What prompts this dissent? In what ways could we strengthen the presentation of the authentic teachings of the magisterium?

- Say "immorality" and most people think of sexual sins. Should we try to broaden public awareness of immorality to include unjust wages, oppression of the poor, racial and sexual discrimination, imbalance of wealth between people and nations? What are other examples of "immorality?"

- Are we only against sin and injustice or can we creatively promote public morality? Decide on one thing your family, group or parish could do to promote public morality—and then do it!

Decision

To strengthen our community to overcome apathy toward sin in society and to help strengthen our family, parish and community, we will _____

_____

_____

_____

_____

_____ .

Prayer

Lord, help us to embrace truth and justice, to live morally and to help change social values that subject people to the indignities of poverty, prejudice and sin. Amen.

Chapter Four

The Sacraments—
God with Us

"Is there anyone sick among you? He should ask for the presbyters of the church. They in turn are to pray over him, anointing him with oil in the Name [of the Lord]. This prayer uttered in faith will reclaim the one who is ill, and the Lord will restore him to health. If he has committed any sins, forgiveness will be his" (see Jas. 5:14-16a).

One day my wife overheard a discussion between two of our grandchildren. Six-year-old Jamie told Philip, her nine-year-old brother, "Mama and Daddy spend all their money on us."

Philip replied, with that impish grin, "I know, but it gives them such pleasure!"

God, our Father, gives us everything—and I think it gives him great pleasure to do so. He created us and all things out of love. When we look at a sunset or a sunrise, a rosebud, a baby's smile, we get a glimpse of how much he loves us.

Sometimes when away from home, I stand at my hotel window in the early morning—ten, twenty or thirty stories high—and watch the city gradually wake up.

First the sky begins to lighten. Shortly before sunup, taxis and public service vehicles, as well as an occasional police car, begin to move along the streets. Then pedestrians come out of their apartment houses or alleys, walking purposefully or stumbling drunkenly along. Gradually, more cars and trucks speed down and up the streets, until, about an hour after sunup, the city is again fully awake, the streets are jammed with traffic and the sidewalks alive with people, like so many ants, scurrying to and fro in search of livelihood.

I think of my own city, my own scurrying, my own haste and waste. I think of God.

The world around us is full of signs and symbols— signs of life, signs of love, signs of power.

I look upon the world and see God; but with all the beauty and wonder in nature and technology, there is in them only a cloudy revelation of God. We can never know God only through creation. That's why he chose to speak personally to us, to become one of us that we might know him and love him.

The God of the Bible, the God of Jesus Christ, the God of the Christian churches has "signed" his creation so that we may be *aware* of him if only we open our eyes and minds. We come to *know* him, however, only through direct revelation.

He has come to us through the prophets, through Scripture. He enters the world as a man in Jesus of Nazareth. He continues his life among us in his Church. Through faith and inspiration, we come to know him and share in his divine life and love.

A sacrament is, according to the old "Baltimore Catechism," an "outward sign of inward grace." The difference between a sign and a sacrament is this: the sign represents or points to a reality, while a sacrament is actually the reality it represents. An exit sign in the theater is not the means of escape in case of a fire. The sign only points to the door which is the means of escape. In a Protestant communion service, the bread and wine (or grape juice) are truly only symbols or signs pointing to the reality of Jesus Christ. In the Catholic Church, because of the action of the Holy Spirit through the ordained priesthood, bread and wine actually become what they signify—the Real Presence of Jesus Christ, in all his humanity and divinity. When we receive Communion, it is no longer bread and wine that we receive—although they appear and taste like bread and wine—but the resurrected, living and glorified Jesus Christ, the only Son of God.

Theologians have written volumes on the depth and breadth of the meaning of sacrament.

The sacraments are the most perfect way in which God touches us and lets us "see" him more clearly. By his own divine will, he "inhabits" the sacramental actions of the Church, gives them life, and makes them real encounters with himself and the entire communion of saints, both living and dead. Catholics who frequent confession and Communion find it easier to keep their minds focused on Jesus, resist temptation and overcome habitual sin.

God's Role and Ours

Because the sacraments are encounters with God, the Church insists on proper preparation for reception of those sacraments.

It is true that, in Baptism for example, a person does not always have to understand what is happening in order to receive the graces and benefits of the sacrament.

An infant does not understand Baptism—but a baptized infant is indeed baptized, filled with the Holy Spirit, cleansed of original sin, made a child of God and a member of the Church.

Many years ago, the infant was given all the sacraments of initiation at one time—Baptism, Confirmation and Eucharist. Those children, even though they did not understand what they were receiving, were being touched and transformed by their God.

Some people argue against infant baptism. They say it can't really do the child any good because he doesn't know what's going on. But these same people will argue that an infant, and even an unborn child, can inherit his rich grandfather's fortune. An infant heir doesn't know he's rich, but he's rich. An infant baptized in Christ doesn't know he's baptized, but he is.

Baptism is God's action, not ours. It is God's gift, not ours. True, we ask adults to learn more about God and the Church before we baptize them. They have reached the age of reason and can use their minds to accept or reject Christ and his Church—but even adults, ignorant of the Catholic faith, are baptized when they are in danger of death or too retarded to learn the basics.

The Church, however, does not administer the sacraments indiscriminately. Under ordinary circumstances, a baby will not be baptized unless the parents are willing to commit themselves to at least a minimum practice of their Catholic faith and agree to attend baptism preparation classes.

Before receiving First Penance (confession) and Eucharist (Communion), both adults and children are prepared. While the sacraments are God's gift to us, when we are old enough and alert enough we must prepare ourselves to understand better his gift and try to give ourselves to him as well.

The "sacraments of commitment" require even more preparation, since they involve mature decision to answer a specific call from God to a special life of love and service. The Church will not permit people to marry or ordain men in Holy Orders unless they are adequately prepared.

Everyone is aware that men seeking ordination to priesthood or diaconate enter long-term formation and training programs. (Men and women entering religious life have a long period for preparation, although their vocation is not a sacrament.)

For too many years, there was little preparation required for marriage, although marriage is a sacrament. It seems as though it was almost considered a "second class" sacrament.

Things are different today. In dioceses throughout the world greater efforts are being made to prepare people for sacramental marriage.

In Florida, for example, all seven dioceses follow the same guidelines for marriage preparation. Couples in which at least one party is under nineteen years of age must receive special counseling before the Church will witness their marriages. Marriages are not permitted just because the girl or woman is pregnant. Each couple seeking a sacramental marriage must come to the Church four months before the date they desire to marry. They participate in one of several examinations which help them surface problem areas in their relationships. They are required to attend Engaged Encounter or Pre-Cana classes. Until all requirements have been met, the couple is not allowed to schedule the wedding date. Sometimes, the couple is asked to postpone the wedding for sake of further reflection, counseling and spiritual preparation.

The Catholic Church believes that sacramental marriages are binding for life and that it is better to help people prepare for marriage—or even decide not to marry—rather than let them enter marriage poorly prepared for the sacrifice and commitment which marriage demands.

To understand all seven sacraments better, we must realize that they are not isolated, unrelated experiences. Each sacrament is integral to the Catholic Christian's entire sacramental life, experience of God and totality of relationships. Baptism, Eucharist, Confirmation, Holy Orders, Holy Matrimony, Penance, Anointing of the Sick—all are expressions of the same wonderful mystery of "God-with-us."

Our Seven Sacraments

Let's take a brief look at each of our seven sacraments.

In *Baptism*, we have original sin washed away and we are filled with God's Spirit. We become children of God and members of the Church. We become heirs of the kingdom, brothers and sisters of Jesus Christ, children of Mary and disciples to carry the Good News throughout the earth.

St. Cyril of Jerusalem lived in the fourth century. In the *Liturgy of the Hours* (Catholic Book Publishing Co., Book III, page 445), the great bishop writes:

"If there is any slave of sin here present, he should at once prepare himself through faith for the rebirth into the freedom that makes us God's adopted children. He should lay aside the wretchedness of slavery to sin, and put on the joyful slavery of the Lord, so as to be counted worthy to inherit the kingdom of heaven.... Through faith receive the Holy Spirit, so that you may be welcomed into the everlasting dwelling

places…. Become a member of Christ's holy and spiritual flock, so that one day you may be set apart on his right hand, and so gain the life prepared as your inheritance.''

In *Confirmation,* we are strengthened again with the Holy Spirit, given a greater share in the ministry of the Church, called to shoulder responsibility for our own faith and to strengthen others in faith. We are called to let the Spirit of God work in our lives, to let him turn our weakness into strength, our timidity into boldness, our short-sightedness into greater vision, our hesitancy and fear into zeal and courage.

In *Eucharist,* Jesus brings us to the foot of his cross to witness, in our own day, our personal and corporate redemption.

Jesus is risen from the dead, ascended into heaven and eternally present before the Father; everything he did on earth is before the Father; at Mass, we enter into the eternal and divine reality of the glorified Jesus. In the Mass, Jesus draws us into himself. We become part of the wonder and horror of Calvary—and of the glory of the resurrection! We are present at our own redemption.

The Eucharist is the center of our faith; it is the living Jesus, in all his humanity and divinity. We become one with him. The God who created everything out of nothing comes to us as food for both body and soul. In Eucharist, we are nourished, forgiven, healed, called and sent.

Not everyone believes in the real presence.

A certain evangelical church that is well known throughout North America produces a stage musical about the life of Jesus. Normally that sect staunchly maintains the inerrancy of the Bible as well as literal interpretation of the Bible.

I was stunned to hear, from the mouth of the actor playing Jesus at the Last Supper: "Take this and eat it for it is a *symbol* of my body."

A symbol? Read any of the gospels and try to find Jesus saying that the Eucharist is a "symbol." This evangelical church, which preaches literal interpretation of scripture and the inerrancy of the Bible, *edited the words of Jesus* to fit its own notions of what Jesus meant at the Last Supper.

Jesus said, "This is my body," and he meant it.

Look at the sixth chapter of the Gospel of John. When Jesus told the people they would have to eat his body and drink his blood to have everlasting life, many people left him. But he did not tell them they had misunderstood him. He did not say, "Oh, I was just talking figuratively, symbolically." No, he let them leave and then asked his apostles, "Are you going to leave me too?" And it was Peter who said, "Lord, to whom shall we go? You have the words of everlasting life."

What a prophetic pronouncement: "You have the words of everlasting life!"

In other words, Peter is telling Jesus, "Lord, what you just said and promised is the key to everlasting life, the way in which we can be sure to be with you in paradise."

My belief in the real presence of Jesus in the Eucharist helped me during a very challenging time.

Back in 1968, when Pope Paul VI published his encyclical, *Humanae Vitae*, hardly anyone paid attention to the entire document. All that most people, including the press, were interested in was the fact that the Holy Father had reaffirmed the magisterium's teaching against artificial birth control. This beautiful document got a bad press. Actually, as its title says, it is a document *On Human Life*. Taken as a whole, it provides the Church's rationale for protecting all of human life, upholds the sacredness of human love and sex in marriage and pronounces that sex in marriage has two goals—the procreation of life and the strengthening of the love and unity of husband and wife.

In 1968, I did not read the document all that carefully myself. I had been sure the pope would change the Church's traditional teaching—and I was bitterly disappointed when he did not.

Many people talked about "walking"—in other words, leaving the Church. I was truly tempted to do so myself, but after some reflection, prayer and counseling, I finally wrote a column entitled, "To Whom Shall We Go?" Had it not been for the Eucharist, I might well have left the Church at that time. I had believed what others had said, that the Church's teaching was antiquated and it would have to be changed because it could not stand up to the experience of good, Catholic married couples and the findings of many modern theologians.

As disappointed as I was with the Holy Father's decision, I knew that I could not find the Eucharist anywhere except in that Church which, through apostolic succession, had the power to change bread and wine into the Body and Blood of the Lord Jesus Christ. In no other Church but the Roman Catholic Church would I have the security and protection of the Chair of Peter, the sign of Jesus' living authority in his true Church.

Our Lord is so gentle. He took me as I was, gave me a deep faith in his presence in the Eucharist, forgave me my sins and led me gradually, to the point that, today, I am totally convinced that the Holy Father's ban on artificial birth control is right and from God.

You can find healing and salvation in the Eucharist—because in Communion you meet the same Jesus who walked the Holy Land; who cured the sick, blind and lame; who forgave people their sins and raised people from the dead.

Think about it! If Jesus walked into your presence right now, wouldn't you believe he had the power to help you? Of course you would. Faith tells us that in Eucharist

Jesus does "walk into our presence" and is there waiting for you and for me, to love us, heal us, forgive us and teach us.

If you don't believe that, pray for the faith to believe.

In *Holy Matrimony*, a man and woman come before their priest and parish community to exchange vows. They make a public statement. They tell each other, the Church and all society that from that day forward they are going to be a living testimony to God's redeeming love.

Marriage is not a private matter. It is a public statement of faith, a missionary statement. To develop a deeper understanding of the Church's teachings on marriage, I suggest reflecting prayerfully on the Vatican Council II *Decree on the Apostolate of Lay People*, and on Pope John Paul's *Apostolic Exhortation on the Family*, both of which may be obtained from the Daughters of St. Paul, 50 St. Paul's Avenue, Boston, MA 02130.

Marriage is as much a Christian commitment and sacrament as is Holy Orders. Marriage, though in a way different from the Eucharist, is the real presence of Jesus. Man and woman become one flesh as God wants his entire people to become one with him in mind and spirit.

A sacramentally married couple is a eucharistic sign in the world. As explained earlier, they embody God's pledge to forever love his people, they bring into their families and the world the redeeming love of Christ and, because they love without reservation, they proclaim that Christ is who he says he is and that he will indeed come again as he has promised.

A commitment to marry is a commitment to society as well as to the Church. Faithful and happily married couples give stability to their families, which give stability to society.

In Holy Matrimony, a man and woman promise to love one another in an exclusive way. They concentrate their love and grace on one another and their family for the sake of Christian witness and the welfare of all the world.

———————————

Holy Orders, like matrimony, is not sufficiently understood or appreciated by most people today. People give their bishops, priests and deacons "job descriptions" and stop there. By defining ordained ministry only by its functions, Catholics make it difficult to appreciate fully the power and blessing of this sacrament.

Deacons, priests and bishops are something more than men who have particular duties and powers such as preaching and proclaiming the gospel and, for priests and bishops, absolving people from sin and presiding at Eucharist.

Holy Orders, like Holy Matrimony, is a "sacrament of commitment." An ordained man gives himself to the entire community. He does not primarily or exclusively concentrate his love on one person and family. God's call to him (and to religious men and women as well) is to give himself to the larger family of the Church, to help prepare God's people for their role in calling the world to Christ.

The deacon's call is also to the entire community, but in a different way. Transitional deacons are men on their way to the priesthood. Permanent deacons are men selected to serve as deacons, most of whom are married, but are not on their way to becoming priests. They are permanent deacons. The Church ordains these men to serve out their lives as deacons because the Order of Deacons is a viable, necessary and powerful ministry in the Church.

The first deacons were ordained by the apostles themselves, after seven men had been selected by the Christian community to serve the needs of the poor (see Acts 6:1-6).

The diaconate is not a "step toward the priesthood," as we had come to believe when the permanent diaconate fell into oblivion many years ago. Rather, the deacon shares in the bishop's priesthood and mission in a very special way.

The priest is ordained to be an extension of the bishop as presider and overseer. The priest, or presbyter (which comes from the Greek, *presbyteros*), presides at Eucharist and pastors a given congregation. The deacon (which comes from the Greek, *diákonos*, which means one who serves) is the bishop's eyes and ears in the community which lives in the world. He is supposed to serve the people of God. He represents the bishop's commitment to meet the needs of the people, in a special way of the poor and otherwise needy. The deacon represents the entire Church's call to loving service.

Both deacons and priests share in the sacrament of Holy Orders, but they are in different orders. It is not correct or fair to consider the priest somehow "more ordained" than the deacon. It is wrong to consider the deacon some kind of "mini-priest" or "glorified altar boy."

Both priest and deacon have their specific share in the bishop's priesthood, which is in turn a share in the priesthood of Jesus Christ.

Holy Orders, no less and no more than Holy Matrimony, is a call to a covenant relationship. This is true for both priests and deacons. First, the priest.

In marriage, husband and wife are covenanted. A priest and his parishioners are also covenanted. There is a lovely ceremony, which too few people ever get to see, for the installation of a new pastor in a parish. The pastor has to pledge obedience to the bishop and the magisterium, and he also pledges to love and serve his people as Christ loves and serves his bride, the Church.

The relationship between parish priest and parishioners can be compared with the relationship between a husband and wife. We can even apply St. Paul's teachings on marriage to the "marriage" of a priest and his people.

Read Ephesians 5:22ff. In our little reflection, the pastor and other parish priests become the husband figure who lays down his life so that his wife (the parishioners) may be made holy. The parishioners submit all things (their time, talent and treasure) to the pastor for the sake of the parish mission, which is to bring Jesus into the world. Their gift is given to the Church for sake of its entire mission, not just for maintenance of parish programs. The energies and resources of the laity are to be spent in bringing the gospel to the secular community—on the job, in civic organizations and through the media.

The married permanent deacon, for his part, is like a man with two wives. There is a constant tension which comes from dividing his attention between his marriage and his ministry in the Church and in the world. If the deacon and his wife do not have a good, strong marriage, if they do not share the sense of mission, then the marriage will be damaged and the ministry terribly weakened.

In most dioceses, wives of men seeking ordination are required to go through the entire formation program with their husbands. They are regarded, in the diaconal community, as an integral part of the deacon's ministry of love and service.

The deacon, if he is properly disposed and trained, comes to his ministry in the Church and world with a tremendous advantage.

He already knows what it means to live a sacrament and to live in covenant. Through the grace they receive as husband and wife, in a sacramental marriage, the deacon and his wife stand in the community as a sign of what the Church is called to become—a community of love dedicated to the service of others.

Peg and I, with Father Ray Larsen, a co-director of the diaconate in our Diocese of Orlando, wrote a paper called, *Marriage and Orders, Sacraments of Commitment in the Mystery of Human Love.*

The paper is a discussion and reflection on how Holy Matrimony and Holy Orders work together in the lives and ministry of the deacon and his wife. Together, we suggest that the permanent diaconate should be regarded more and more as the Church's ordained ministry *in the world*, and that the permanent deacon should become the recognized minister of people in their work-a-day situation, the minister who helps inspire and enable them to live Christian lives and bear Christian witness in the world, the minister who, perhaps more than any other ordained minister, knows how to preach the gospel in secular situations.

This understanding of diaconate may well be an answer to the need which prompted experiments with "worker priests" in some countries a few years ago.

However, we must not be too exclusive. The priest never ceases to be a deacon. The bishop never ceases to be a priest and a deacon. All ordained ministers are called to a life of loving service for God and witness to the gospel for the entire world.

We are speaking here of primary calls, signs, ministries.

We will never understand the priesthood (or the priesthood of the faithful, which we all enter at baptism) if we limit our understanding of priesthood to the inner workings and ministry of the Church.

It is true that the parish priest is called to serve his own people—but the people he is serving are commanded by Jesus Christ to be missionaries in their world. No priest can adequately serve his people and no people can adequately respond to priestly ministry if the parish is not concerned with bringing new life into the Church, of preaching the gospel in the marketplace, of inviting the unchurched into the family of faith.

No deacon is called to serve the Church only in the world. He has liturgical responsibilities. He is, as much as the priest, a preacher of homilies, a presider over liturgies other than the Eucharist, an ordinary minister of Baptism. He can witness marriages and bury the dead.

The priest, who never ceases to be a deacon, is empowered also to preside at the Mass, to consecrate the bread and wine, to absolve people from their sins. Under special circumstances, and with the permission of his bishop, the priest can also administer the sacrament of Confirmation.

The bishop never ceases to be deacon and priest. He is further empowered to ordain men to the diaconate, the priesthood and the episcopacy.

While we must never forsake the hierarchy the Lord gave his Church, we must never smother the creative power of God in responses proposed to meet certain needs in certain times. We must be open to the Spirit and recognize God's gift in all ordained ministries.

Today's diaconate, I believe, is part of God's answer to the needs of our own times—not because there is a shortage of priests, but because there is a great need for an organized commitment to preaching in the marketplace, a commitment, that in our tradition is best expressed when ordained ministers are part of the picture.

The *Sacrament of Reconciliation*, also called Penance or Confession, is a wonderful gift from God to help people experience and encounter their healing and forgiving God.

Sister Briege McKenna's book, *Miracles Do Happen*, recounts many stories in which people's lives have been changed through this magnificent sacrament. As co-author of that book I have received many calls from people throughout the world who, because they finally asked, have experienced the presence of God in their lives.

One man came to visit me from another country. He told me that he had stopped going to church many years ago. A relative sent him a copy of Sister Briege's book. He read it and was deeply moved. He tried to reach Sister Briege and could not, so he picked up her book again and thought, "Maybe she'll talk to me through this book." He opened the book randomly and his eyes fell on a story about a young man who had fallen away from the Church. Sister Briege had told the young man to go to confession. He did and had a tremendous experience of spiritual renewal. He felt the presence of God.

This man said he felt sure he, too, was supposed to go to confession. He did, and he also experienced a deep spiritual healing.

He had come to see me, first of all because Sister Briege was not available, and secondly because he wanted his life changed even further. He wanted a miracle, even if the miracle was only the strength to accept certain things in his life that he could not change.

We prayed together—and the Lord touched us both deeply.

After we prayed, he was like a new man. His face radiated peace and his eyes shone brightly. His step was lighter and his attitude more positive.

Because he obeyed the inspiration to go to confession, this man felt the healing touch of Jesus. He gained the courage to do what seemed very foolish—to travel many hundreds of miles to meet a stranger to talk about his experience and to pray.

Because of his positive response to the promptings of the Holy Spirit, this man now has a deep desire to get to know Jesus better. He marvels at what God has done in the lives of other people. He wants to be transformed—and if he continues to pray and put God first, if he continues to humble himself before God, confess his sins and do penance, he will be transformed.

Transformation comes through obedience. Through the Church, Jesus has told us we must confess our sins to the priest. The priest has no magical powers. He has the power of Christ. He is the representative of Christ and the Church when he administers the sacraments. In confession, when he says, "I absolve you..." it is Jesus absolving, assuring you through his living Body, the Church, that you are forgiven.

Even our most private sins weaken the Church, since we are the Church. The Sacrament of Reconciliation is the way we tell both God and the Church that we are sorry. The sacrament is the way in which God and the Church say, "That's okay. You're forgiven. Let's continue to love one another and work for the salvation of souls."

There is today a tremendous disaffection among Catholics for this great sacrament. Sometimes people argue that private confession to the priest was not always the rule, and so it cannot be all that important. It is true that the present form of celebrating Reconciliation developed only in the eleventh or twelfth century—but it has roots in the very heart of Jesus and in the early Church.

After his resurrection, Jesus laid hands on his disciples, breathed on them and said, "Receive the Holy Spirit. If you forgive men's sins, they are forgiven them; if you hold them bound, they are held bound" (Jn. 20:23).

Very early in the Church, it was recognized that even after baptism people sinned and there had to be some way in which repentance and forgiveness could be recognized and celebrated. Public confession became the way people apologized to God and the Church—and penances, rather harsh ones, were imposed.

Later, private confession developed—confession to a pastor of the Church, one who had the authority from Christ to forgive sin in Jesus' name and in the name of the Church.

One more point. The Holy Father and the bishops have both authority and power to teach. We have the guarantee from Jesus that his Church will not teach anything that is not morally and doctrinally correct. These teachers are telling us, in the name of Jesus, that private confession is the proper way to celebrate penance in our time. This could change at another time, but it is not changing now.

If we are to be obedient to Christ, we must obey the pastors he has placed over us, for he speaks through them.

It is not easy to tell another person your sins—but in the confessional, if you wish, you can go to confession behind a screen, preserving your anonymity.

In confession, you receive healing and you don't have to pay the $100 an hour a psychiatrist would charge. In confession, you get assurance that your sins are forgiven. In therapy, you may learn behavior modification and begin to think better of yourself. With a Christian therapist, you may even learn to love God, others and self more—but it is only in confession that we are absolutely guaranteed, and can celebrate the fact, that our sins are forgiven.

Go to confession. Please. You need it and the Church needs you.

———————

A wonderful thing happened in our own parish of St. Mary Magdalen in Altamonte Springs, FL. The priests of the parish had a communal *Anointing of the Sick*. This beautiful liturgy includes scripture readings, a homily and individual administration of the anointing of the sick.

One woman had come for anointing. She did not really believe she could be healed. She was going blind and the doctors had said there was no hope for her, that in one year's time she would be totally, permanently blind.

She was anointed and shortly afterwards moved north again.

More than a year later, she returned for a visit and told a parishioner what had happened. She had been completely healed. Her eyesight was better than ever.

The Anointing of the Sick used to be known as the Last Rites or Extreme Unction. Since the Second Vatican Council, we have tried to recapture the understanding of the early Church, that in the anointing of the sick, Jesus is present with his healing power.

The quote from the letter of James used at the beginning of this chapter supports our sacrament of Anointing of the Sick.

After years of receiving the sacraments, we can begin to take them for granted, to forget the great miracle of God's ministering presence in these wonderful encounters with him in his Church.

There was a certain man who for many years didn't like any organized religion because each one "puts God in a bottle and says, 'Here he is! This is God and nobody else's idea of God is correct, only ours!'"

He was a Catholic but no longer practiced his faith because he saw the Catholic Church as "just one other Church claiming to have God all bottled up."

Later, the man experienced a wonderful and startling insight. "In the sacraments," he suddenly realized, "God puts himself in a bottle so his children can touch him and begin to know him."

And with that, let's reflect on the sacraments. Our examination of conscience here will not be based on the Ten Commandments, but on our response to the Lord in the "ordinary."

For Personal Reflection

Scripture

"Jesus took bread, blessed it, broke it, and gave it to his disciples. 'Take this and eat it,' he said, 'this is my body.' Then he took a cup, gave thanks, and gave it to them. 'All of you must drink from it,' he said, 'for this is my blood, the blood of the covenant, to be poured out in behalf of many for the forgiveness of sins...'" (Mt. 26:26-28).

Prayer

Lord, I know that you are real and that you love me. But I get so overwhelmed with daily concerns that I do not recognize you in the ordinary ways in which you come to me—in the love of spouse, children and friends. It's even hard, sometimes, to realize you are truly present in the sacraments. They seem so ordinary. Help me Jesus to recognize you in the people around me and help me to develop a deep faith in your presence and ministry in the sacraments.

Examination of Conscience

(This examination of conscience reviews personal attitudes toward all seven sacraments. It is a little longer than the other reflections. The reader may want to provide a little more time for adequate reflection.)

(Remember to use your notebook to record special insights and ideas.)

1. God is present to me every day in so many ways. His beauty and glory are manifest in nature, in sunrises and sunsets, at mountainsides and seashores, in other people and in the Church.

• Do I take time to see God in nature? In other words, do I take time out to smell the roses?

- Do I see God in other people—in someone poking along in the car ahead of me, or in the person trying to find a Christian who will let him enter the heavy traffic on a busy road?

2. The Church is the "eighth sacrament," the real presence of Jesus in the world.

- How can I, as a member of God's family, bring his love and goodness to others? What are my special gifts, my talents?

- Do I regard others, especially those who rub me the wrong way, as brothers and sisters?

3. Jesus is truly present in all the sacraments.

- Through Baptism, I was cleansed of original sin and became a child of God. Do I reflect on the gift of my own baptism? Do I attend baptisms in my parish to show parents that our parish is a Christian family upon whom they can depend?

- Through Confirmation, I was confirmed in the power of the Holy Spirit, anointed with chrism and given the duty and privilege to share my Catholic, Christian faith with others. Do I pray to the Holy Spirit to keep the grace of Baptism and Confirmation alive in my heart so I can and will be a witness for Jesus and a friend of all I meet?

- Through Eucharist, as I consume the host, I am consumed by the fiery love of Jesus, the Father and the Holy Spirit. Do I believe that the Jesus I receive in Eucharist is the same Jesus who forgave and healed so many years ago? Do I believe he wants to touch me, heal me and let me experience his love right now?

- Jesus heals and forgives in the Sacrament of Reconciliation (confession). Do I confess regularly? If not, what is there about the sacrament, or about me, that stands in the way of this wonderful encounter with Jesus?

- In Holy Matrimony, a man and woman become one heart, mind and flesh. Do I respect this sacrament as a beautiful way in which God takes on flesh in the world and the redeeming love of Jesus is made present in the world? If I am married, do I pray with my spouse for God to strengthen our union and make us a vibrant sign of his love in our family, parish and community? Am I faithful to my vocation and do I respect others in theirs?

- In Holy Orders, men are called to serve God by serving the people of God and the people of the world. Do I see bishops, priests and deacons first of all as brothers who share the same baptismal faith in Christ? Or rather than looking at the mystery of Christ's ministerial presence in them, do I place them in neat little categories according to the jobs they do? Do I pray for vocations to the priesthood and diaconate—and, at the same time, to the religious life?

- The Church administers the Sacrament of the Anointing of the Sick to make present to each of us the healing power of Jesus Christ. Do I have faith enough to realize that Jesus heals through this sacrament in the way that I most need to be healed? Am I open to the power of God to heal physically as well as spiritually? Do I realize that forgiveness of sin and reconciliation with God and Church is the greatest healing of all?

4. In what ways can I increase my appreciation for God's presence in life, in the Church and in the sacraments? (Add your own ideas to these suggestions:)

- Take five minutes every day just to look at the world around you.

- Go to a weekday Mass at least once a week.

- Attend parish baptisms.

- Before Mass begins, spend a few minutes reflecting on the gift of Eucharist.

- Go to confession at least once a month.

Decision
    To become more aware of God's presence in the ordinary people and events of my daily life and in the sacraments, I will _____

_____

_____

_____

_____

_____

_____.

Prayer
    Jesus, I want to recognize you in life, in others and in the Church and her sacraments. Please help me organize my life around you. Give me the grace to make time for roses, sunsets, the needy, the lonely and the anxious. As you reach through me to others, Lord, please touch, bless and heal me, too. Amen.

For Shared Reflection

Scripture

"The eleven disciples made their way to Galilee, to the mountain to which Jesus had summoned them. At the sight of him, those who had entertained doubts fell down in homage. Jesus came forward and addressed them in these words:

"'Full authority has been given to me
both in heaven and on earth;
go, therefore, and make disciples of all nations.
Baptize them in the name
"of the Father and of the Son,
and of the Holy Spirit."
"'Teach them to carry out everything I have
commanded you.
And know that I am with you always, until the end
of the world!'" (Mt. 28:16-20)

Prayer

Lord Jesus, it is difficult to understand how we can be your presence on earth. We have our own doubts and make many mistakes. We often lack true charity and unity in our Christian relationships. Yet, Lord, we want to improve, to grow, to be forgiven and to be healed. Help us to become a family you can be proud of, a family that will love so many so well that your Church will grow in holiness and in members. Amen.

Discussion Starters

1. Let each person share, from his or her individual reflection, what special thing he or she will do to learn to seek the Lord in the ordinary.

2. In our parish, are there ways in which we can make the celebration of the sacraments more meaningful to more people?

3. Are baptisms, confirmations, marriages and ordinations recognized as occasions for the entire parish family to praise God and rejoice with one another?

4. In what ways are we, as a parish family, the "eighth sacrament," the presence of God in our own local community? In what ways can we become a more effective presence in our own community? Here are some ideas. Please add your own.

Social issues:

- Show parishioners that helping people "in the world" is both a personal and community responsibility: by participating in community efforts to provide housing, food and clothing for the needy; and by offering leadership in fighting drug and alcohol addiction as well as other public problems.

- Help the members of our parish and the community at large to understand that the poor need help year-round and not just at Easter, Thanksgiving and Christmas.

Liturgical concerns:

- Make an effort to encourage more parishioners to be present at baptisms, confirmations, weddings and ordinations.

- Re-educate parishioners about the need and beauty of confession and the social nature of sin. Hold penance services which will encourage people to take advantage of private confession.

- Reflect on our liturgy to see how we can improve our Sunday worship through the training and spiritual formation of the parish ministers of Word, Eucharist, music and hospitality (ushers).

Decision

To help our local community and ourselves become

more conscious of God's presence in our lives, we will

_____

_____

_____

_____

_____

_____

_____.

Prayer

There are many challenges, Jesus, and we want to meet them in a way that increases the honor and glory you receive from all peoples. Please bless our pastors, deacons, religious and lay ministers—and all of us. Give us your Spirit and a desire to increase our parish awareness of your presence in our Church, in our sacraments and in our ministry in the world. Amen.

Chapter Five

Do Whatever He Tells You: Finding Joy in Pleasing God

"In the sixth month, the angel Gabriel was sent from God to a town of Galilee named Nazareth, to a virgin betrothed to a man named Joseph, of the house of David. The virgin's name was Mary. Upon arriving, the angel said to her: 'Rejoice, O highly favored daughter! The Lord is with you. Blessed are you among women.... You have found favor with God. You shall conceive and bear a son and give him the name Jesus. Great will be his dignity and he will be called Son of the Most High....'

"Mary said to the angel, 'How can this be since I do not know man?' The angel answered her: 'The Holy Spirit will come upon you and the power of the Most High will overshadow you; hence, the holy offspring to be born will be called Son of God'" (Lk.1:26-35).

A woman experienced two major tragedies within a few short months. Both her husband and only son died. Her life had already been filled with difficulties.

These tragedies, in the mind of her pastor, must have been entirely too much to bear.

In an effort to comfort the woman, the priest said, "I really wish I could tell you why this has happened."

The woman replied, "Father, never ask 'Why?' That is a stupid question because there is no answer for it. I'm not asking, 'Why did this happen to me?' I'm asking, 'Given my faith in Jesus, what am I going to do now? How am I going to respond to this in my life?'"

This woman's attitude goes beyond simply wanting to overcome sin. She has decided to follow Jesus and to respond to life as he responded—in love and compassion. Surely, she continues to struggle against her own tendency to fail, but her vision is focused on total, personal transformation, on pleasing God.

Her presence of mind in such overwhelming difficulties calls to mind a beautiful scene from Mark's Gospel in which the serenity of Jesus and the shallow faith of his disciples are clearly contrasted.

"Leaving the crowd, they took [Jesus] away in the boat in which he was sitting, while the other boats accompanied him. It happened that a bad squall blew up. The waves were breaking over the boat and it began to ship water badly. Jesus was in the stern through it all, sound asleep on a cushion. They finally woke him and said to him, 'Teacher, does it not matter to you that we are going to drown?' He awoke and rebuked the wind and said to the sea: 'Quiet! Be still!' The wind fell off and everything grew calm. Then he said to them, 'Why were you so terrified? Why are you lacking in faith?' A great awe overcame them at this. They kept saying to one another, 'Who can this be that the wind and sea obey him?'" (Mk. 4:36-41)

Jesus had faith in his Father. His faith had two major characteristics. First, he knew the Father. Second, he was one with his Father in love. Knowing the Father intimately, Jesus could "rest in him," so to speak. He was confident that his Father would care for him.

That confidence and trust, expressed so many times throughout his life, would stand by him in Gethsemane, when, with great fear and trepidation he would beg his Father to take away his cross. His faith and trust would enable him to say, "But your will, not mine, be done."

The image of Jesus asleep on a cushion in the back of the boat is a great help to finding joy in pleasing God.

Obedience and Joy

Obedience, when motivated by love, brings great joy. Obedience, when motivated by fear, brings depression.

A husband and wife who love one another have little difficulty remaining faithful. Each lives for the other. The loved one is the all important person in life.

I have seen hundreds of women, for example, who spend themselves tirelessly for their husbands and children.

One in particular, a woman in her mid-80s, was still keeping house for a son and daughter-in-law who were both in poor health. She acted as chauffeur, cook, washerwoman, counselor, friend, teacher.

She never once complained and when friends suggested she was out of her mind doing all that at her age, she would say simply, "They need me. I can do it, and they can't, so I do it."

She loved.

In the early 1970s, a group of Cajuns in the Orlando area decided to host a "Cajun Day" for all Cajuns living in that area. They planned to have Cajun food and Cajun records to dance by.

They thought maybe fifty or sixty people would show up. They had no idea how many Cajuns were living in the Orlando area. Advance registrations numbered 800 people coming to "Cajun Day."

One of the Orlando Cajuns knew a cook in Lafayette, LA who loved to cook for big crowds. The man came to the rescue of the local group.

The media covered the day quite extensively. One radio reporter interviewed the chef and asked him, "What prompted you to come all this way to cook for all these people?" If the reporter was waiting for some profound philosophical answer, he was disappointed. The man from Louisiana said simply and with all candor, "Because I wanted to."

I wanted to. I wanted to help out. These are my people and they wanted to celebrate their Cajun heritage and were in over their heads, so I wanted to help them.

The chef may never be able to see or admit that he acted out of love, but he did. In fact, what he did reminds me of the story of Jesus at Cana.

Jesus Responds in Love

The hosts of the wedding feast ran out of wine. Mary told Jesus, "They have no more wine." She told the stewards, "Do whatever he tells you." Jesus changed water into wine. The stewards were surprised and marvelled at the power of Jesus.

Did they experience joy? Perhaps not. But because they did what he told them, even if only out of curiosity or for a selfish reason, they did get an insight into the power of Jesus—and that insight could have motivated them to get to know Jesus better.

We know for certain, however, that this first miracle of Jesus was instrumental in convincing his apostles of his mission and of his divinity.

Peter was handpicked by Jesus to be the prince of the apostles, the man we have come to recognize as our first pope. Yet, he denied Jesus three times out of fear. He truly loved Jesus, but, being human, he succumbed to the instinct of self-preservation at the expense of loyalty, truth and friendship. Peter must have felt as though his actions were almost as bad as those of Judas, who betrayed Jesus.

To Love God Is to Obey Him

But after the resurrection, Jesus gave Peter the opportunity to express his love three times (see Jn. 21:15ff.) and he gave Peter the authority to care for and tend the lambs and the sheep.

History and our own beautiful tradition tell us that because he loved the Lord Peter became a great saint, one who, out of love, obeyed Jesus all the way to his own martyrdom. Peter loved Jesus so much that as he faced death, he told his executioners that he was not worthy to die in the same manner as had Jesus. He asked them to crucify him upside down—and they obliged him.

Read Peter's homily in the second chapter of Acts; live with him as he gives witness to the pagans in the tenth chapter. Listen to Paul after his miraculous conversion on the road to Damascus (see Acts, chapter 9). Throughout all the Acts of the Apostles there runs a thread of unbridled joy in the Lord. There is joy because, through obedience to his word, the apostles and disciples share in his precious and divine life and power. Through obedience in love, they become what they were created to be, sons and daughters of God who give him honor and witness his saving love throughout the world.

How else to overcome habitual sin and to demonstrate love for God than through obedience?

Wisdom is the ultimate gift of the Holy Spirit (see Is. 11:1-11). To me, in my own simple way of looking at things, we have wisdom when we want what God wants.

Jesus possessed wisdom. He was wisdom incarnate. He wanted what the Father wanted—and he was at peace. Jesus was at peace in the storm because he trusted his Father. He was at peace in Gethsemane and on Calvary, because he trusted his Father. And what trust! To believe you are being delivered from death even as you die!

Trust is the twin of hope. When we trust, we become "optimistic" people, we have a certain confidence about the future.

The Jews trusted in God. They knew that God did not lie and they believed that God would send a Messiah to deliver them from oppression. We Christians believe that Jesus is that Messiah. The Jews do not. They are still waiting.

Jesus is the Messiah. He fulfills all the prophesies. The poor and oppressed have the gospel preached to them. They are delivered from bondage and made heirs to the kingdom of heaven. The lame walk, the blind see, the dead are raised.

At the end of World War II there was great joy in our house when we realized that my brother would be coming home. So would all the "boys" who managed to survive that terrible war. But many would never come home. Their sacrifice had helped end the war, had helped preserve freedom.

Jesus' death on the cross won the war against sin and death. Christians who know Jesus personally are excited about their faith. They know that Jesus is real. He is alive. He loves us and lives in us, calling us to fidelity, to liberty from the chains of sin, to a share in his own resurrected glory now and hereafter and in his mission to bring every person into his kingdom.

Faith, Trust and Joy

When Christians truly believe in Jesus, they trust the Father as Jesus trusts the Father. They experience peace—and in peace we find the roots of joy.

Think of what Jesus says in the Gospel of John:

"As the Father has loved me, so I have loved you. Live on in my love. You will live in my love if you keep my commandments, even as I have kept my Father's commandments and live in his love. All this I tell you so that my joy may be yours and your joy may be complete. This is my commandment: love one another as I have loved you" (Jn. 15:9-12).

Jesus commands us to love with his love. He promises joy if we do what he says.

Joy is not happiness. Joy does not depend on luck or outside influences. Joy comes from the deep recesses of a person's mind and heart; it comes from being one with the Lord, from sharing his suffering as well as his glory.

In the first Letter of Peter, we read:

"There is cause for rejoicing here. You may for a time have to suffer the distress of many trials; but this is so that your faith, which is more precious than the passing splendor of fire-tried gold, may by its genuineness lead to praise, glory, and honor when Jesus Christ appears" (1:6-8).

"So gird the loins of your understanding; live soberly; set all your hope on the gift to be conferred on you when Jesus Christ appears. As obedient sons [and

daughters] do not yield to the desires that once shaped you in your ignorance. Rather, become holy yourselves in every aspect of your conduct, after the likeness of the holy One who called you; remember, Scripture says, 'Be holy, for I am holy'" (1:13-16).

"By obedience to the truth you have purified yourselves for a genuine love of your brothers; therefore, love one another constantly from the heart. Your rebirth has come, not from a destructible but from an indestructible seed, through the living and enduring word of God....

"So strip away everything vicious, everything deceitful; pretenses, jealousies, and disparaging remarks of any kind. Be as eager for milk as newborn babies— pure milk of the spirit to make you grow unto salvation, now that you have tasted that the Lord is good.

"Come to him a living stone, rejected by men but approved, nonetheless, and precious in God's eyes. You too are living stones, built as an edifice of spirit, into a holy priesthood, offering spiritual sacrifices acceptable to God through Jesus Christ..." (1:22-23, 2:1-5).

People who think "accepting Jesus as Lord" means the end of all their problems really have another thing coming. Jesus himself said that he had no place in which to lay his head (see Mt. 8:20) and he promised also that if we want to be his disciples, we must each take up his cross daily and follow him (see Mt. 16-24).

A Man Who Loved, Trusted

When I think of people who lived and died in joy, one man stands out in particular. He was Deacon Bud Ward of the Diocese of Orlando.

Bud was a man who truly believed in and loved Jesus. In New York state he had worked among the poor, often traveling alone in areas in which it was extremely dangerous to travel alone. He loved Mary, too, and had been very active in the Legion of Mary, visiting people in their homes to help them discover the joy of knowing Jesus as personal Savior and belonging to him in his Church.

Although Bud and I were not intimate friends, he did have a profound impact on my life. When I was in formation for the diaconate, Bud was dying of cancer. So was his mother-in-law. His wife, Peg, was caring for both of them. Bud continued in ministry, suffering from chemotherapy and from the effects of inoperable cancer of the lungs. He also continued in his work as a manager in a cloth store chain.

One morning, Peg Ward died suddenly, a victim of a heart attack. Bud received people at the wake and assisted at the funeral Mass. His children served as lectors at the Mass.

A few weeks later, Bud's mother-in-law died. Again, Bud, who was himself dying from cancer, comforted everyone else.

Within a few short weeks, Bud himself died, but not until he had shared from the pulpit his hope and joy in his Savior. He said he wanted to live, but he was ready to die. Whatever the Lord wanted was okay with him.

I recall telephoning Bud just a few weeks before his death to comfort him and he ended up giving me a pep talk, in his own quiet and respectful manner, about sticking to my decision to be a deacon. Several of us went to visit Bud just a few days before his death. He was in great pain, but he smiled and spoke of the goodness of the God whom he trusted with all his heart.

He smiled. In pain, and dying, he smiled. Knowing that his twenty-one-year-old son and eighteen-year-old daughter would lose mother, grandmother and father in just three months, he smiled.

What love Bud must have had for Jesus and his family! He knew his Lord so well and loved him so much that he trusted everything to Jesus. He trusted so much that he could smile in the face of pain and death, knowing that God would care for his children. That is the foundation for joy—total love and trust, no matter what.

It is not easy to be faithful. There are indeed many things that distract us from God. Sales managers often tell their sales people, ''Every problem is an opportunity.'' We might adopt that attitude in our quest for peace and joy in God.

Each temptation and distraction is an opportunity to find joy through pleasing God.

Look at Mary, the Mother of Jesus. When the angel appeared to her, she was faced with a momentous decision—to become the mother of Jesus, to be sure, but also an unwed mother, with all the problems that could mean to her in the culture of the day.

Unfaithful women were stoned to death and Mary must have considered that fact in making her decision—and she did have to make a decision. Her mission was not forced on her. She had to agree to become pregnant through the power of God, to chance losing social status, to chance being condemned as a harlot. She had to face Joseph, who loved her so chastely.

Mary decided for God. She decided to please God. ''Behold the handmaid of the Lord.'' I am the servant of the Lord, she said, and whatever he wants, no matter the cost, is what I want.

Then Mary had other decisions, other distractions to overcome.

Here she was, a virgin, with child. Now that would be a curiosity in any society! She had to cope with the miracle, remain humble, put her attention on God and God's Son and not on herself.

Imagine the temptation to sit back and bask in the glory of the moment. "God chose me! God thinks I am special! Goody for me!"

Mary again decided for God's pleasure. She took the angel at his word, believed that her elderly cousin Elizabeth had conceived, and went to visit her, to help her, to be with her, to celebrate the new life each had in her womb.

Mary chose to love, to trust, to be faithful no matter what.

She wanted to please God, and because she made the right choice she could proclaim with all honesty and humility, "My being proclaims the greatness of the Lord, my spirit finds joy in God my savior, for he has looked upon his servant in her lowliness; all ages to come shall call me blessed" (see Lk. 1:46-48).

She had felt the touch of God, had God's life in her. Now her entire being exulted in God, tingled with the presence of God, filled her heart to bursting with joy in God. Surely, in her ecstacy, everything around her must have taken on new beauty. The grass must have been greener, the water cooler and purer, the sky more blue, the breeze more sweet, the flowers more colorful, the day more glorious and other people more lovable. Surely, she must have been conscious of the divinity and wonder of the Life in her womb, a Life so powerful that Elizabeth's John leapt for joy in her own womb at the sound of the wonder-filled and joyful voice of Mary.

If we obey God, we will love and respect all life, we will help people in need, become peacemakers, protect the weak and helpless, call people to conversion by forgiving them the abuses they heap upon us.

If we respond obediently, as did Mary, to God's call to serve him with faith and in trust, life will be more

beautiful. It will be filled with the same joy that transformed all Mary's problems into opportunities and her
opportunities into praise.

Mary is the first Christian and a mother to us all.
Let's take a look at this great woman.

Mary, Winner of Hearts

Many of us were rooted deeply in faith from our
earliest childhood. Those lessons and our memories of
learning about Jesus play an important part in our
continued growth. It is good, occasionally, to think
back to those early days, when the mystery of God's
love was revealed to us through our parents, grandparents or other concerned and loving adults.

As far back as I can remember, what I recall most
vividly is going to Mass with Mama, Daddy and my
brother, Chuck. I remember learning about Jesus and
the Church from my mother. As I sat on the floor at her
feet, she drilled me in the *Baltimore Catechism*.

I remember, too, a certain fascination with my
mother's hands—hands that kneaded dough, sewed
patches on clothes, stirred in pots, hands that daily
fingered the beads of her rosary.

It's a very special rosary. Mama and Daddy lost
several pregnancies and one "blue baby" who lived
only three months. When Mama was carrying me, she
had great difficulty with the pregnancy. Miscarriage
was a constant threat. A nun, whose name Mama never
forgot but I can never remember, gave Mama a rosary.
It was green in color, made of cow horn.

All my life, I remember that rosary—lying on the
nightstand at the head of her bed, resting in her lap on
a Sunday afternoon or clacking gently against the pew
in church.

In 1984, shortly before she died, she complained about not being able to pray anymore. I suddenly found myself the owner of that precious old rosary. The cow horn cross is bent from the pressure of her fingers holding tightly to the symbol of her salvation. The old brass corpus has a broken arm. The original center piece had somehow broken one day, but Daddy carved another one for Mama, also out of cow horn, and made a spare to boot.

That rosary is truly a sacramental. It reminds me of the Lord and our precious Mother Mary, to be sure, but it is a tangible sign, too, of how the faith was passed on to me from my parents. It is a link with my Mama and Daddy who, when I was being knit in secret in her womb, prayed fervently that I might live.

When I was born, Mama nearly died. But God decided it was best that we both live.

I have several rosaries, including a rather unusual one a friend brought me from Medjugorje; but when times are really rough and I need an emotional connection with my faith roots, when I especially need my mother, I take out that old green cow horn rosary and pray. Sometimes, I don't say the prayers of the rosary, but just hold that precious relic and experience a beautiful visit with Jesus, Mary and Mama.

Mary has always been special to us. Except for a time during and immediately following Vatican Council II, when I got too smart for my own good and too big for my britches, I have always had an active devotion to Mary.

When one of our children was near death, it was through the intercession of Mary that he lived. Later, the same child again nearly died, and again, he lived through the intercession of Mary. My wife, Peg, was pregnant with our second daughter when the doctors discovered a rapidly growing kidney stone. She had to have surgery. It would be risky for the baby, but without surgery, the doctors felt that both Peg and the baby would probably die.

She went to the hospital for surgery. She had a reaction to the drugs as they wheeled her into the operating room, before the doctor began his procedure. He came out and said to me, "She's stopped breathing." I nearly fainted. I thought that was his way of saying she had died. As I swooned, he caught me, shook me and said quickly, "No, no, she's alive. We're pumping air into her and helping her breathe. But I have never seen anyone stop breathing this long and live."

He went back into the operating room. I turned away and went down the hall. We had been making novenas to Our Lady of Perpetual Help. As I rounded a corner in Our Lady of Lourdes Hospital in Lafayette, LA, I came face to face with a statue of Mary. All I could think or say was, "Mother of God! Our children!"

I turned back toward the operating room and when I was still a ways from its double doors, the doctor came bursting out all smiles saying, "She's fine. She's fine. She's going to be all right." She had not breathed on her own for nearly two hours.

We went back home for Peg to rest and came back two weeks later. She went through surgery with no ill effects.

Four-and-a-half months later, our biggest, healthiest and sassiest baby was born. A girl. We named her Mary.

In gratitude to our Mother, each of our children, at baptism or confirmation, was named for Mary. We are the proud parents of David Javis Marie, Ray Anthony Marie, Karen Ann Marie, Mary Margaret Marie (she took Mary's name again at confirmation), Suzanne Marie, Angela Marie and Henry Pierre Marie.

All our children are wonderful and generous people. I like to think it's because Mary, the Mother of Jesus and our Mother as well, has been asked and has agreed to take special care of them. Not all of them are as involved in the Church as are their parents, but they all love deeply and sincerely, have wonderful families and make a significant contribution to the world.

Of all our children, I think our son Tony has the most readable heart. He always has his heart in his hand, reaching out to others. He has a spontaneous goodness, a contagious sense of humor. When I look into his eyes, I sometimes also see a sort of sadness. In those special moments, he reminds me of Mary. She was so good and still suffered so much, so generous yet God demanded ever more.

Mary in the Gospels

It is interesting that even Protestants are rediscovering Mary. I have heard of a Lutheran minister who has a statue of Mary and who prays the rosary daily. Even a few fundamentalists are beginning to acknowledge that Mary is really a very special person who deserves our respect and admiration, a person too long ignored.

One author has said that "Protestants are discovering Mary through Scripture and Catholics are rediscovering her in Scripture" (Laurentin, *Queen of Heaven*, p. 37, quoted in *A New Catholic Commentary on Holy Scripture*, Thomas Nelson, Inc., Publishers).

For so many years there was a terrible misunderstanding among Protestants about Catholic devotion to Mary. We still find fundamentalist or evangelical preachers who claim that Catholics worship Mary.

Some Catholics have contributed to the misunderstanding through an exaggerated Marian devotion.

Also, for many years Catholics were not comfortable talking about Jesus, even though they loved him and worshiped him. Catholics felt incompetent in sharing their faith. They did not know Scripture. They had a traditional faith—and Protestants did not appreciate Tradition.

Today, it's different. Catholics are reading Scripture and a growing number can effectively present the truth about Catholic belief.

In their rediscovery of Scripture, Catholics are finding new insights into Mary. I happen to think that the Catholic movement toward Scripture has made it easier for Protestants to listen to Catholic Tradition. "If Catholics are reading the Bible," they may reason, "then we have a common ground on which to discuss Catholic belief."

Whatever the case, Catholics are discovering for themselves, in Scripture, even greater understanding of Mary and her role in salvation history.

As we read and study the gospels, we find the sacred writers only gradually revealing more and more about Mary. However, the earliest mention of Mary in the New Testament, though not by name, was not in a gospel but in one of Paul's letters.

The gospels are thought to have made their appearance in this order: Mark, first; Luke, second; Matthew, third; and John, fourth. If we seek Mary in the gospels in the order in which they were written, we find a growing awareness, in the early Church, of Mary's role and significance in salvation history.

There is a scholarly but readable article in *A New Catholic Commentary on Holy Scripture*. The article, "The Mother of Jesus in the Scriptures," by G. Graystone, M.M., is worth study. It outlines the developing understanding of Mary's role and the similarity of her experience with that of Old Testament women who, though married and not pledged to virginity as was

Mary, also conceived by God's special intervention. We remember especially Sarah (Gn. 17:1-18:15; 21:1-8), Rebekah (Gn. 26:19-26), Samson's mother (Jgs. 13:1-24), and Hannah (1 Sm. 1-28). These are beautiful faith stories and deserve reading and reflection.

From the Annunciation onward, Mary was called into an intimate relationship with her Son, the Messiah. But she had to struggle with that reality without complete and full understanding of what was going on. Scripture tells us that she "pondered" in her heart what she discovered, little by little, about Jesus. At the presentation, when Jesus was a baby, the prophet Simeon proclaimed the holiness and mission of the Babe and told Mary she would experience deep sorrow. When Jesus was found, at age 12, with the wise men in the temple, his parents confronted him with their concern. He told Mary he had to be about his Father's work. She had much to contemplate (see Lk. 2:25ff; 2:41ff.).

When Jesus was about 30 years of age, and apparently Joseph was already dead, Mary saw her Son leave home to begin his public ministry. She must have felt alone. She heard him tell a crowd of people that his real mother, brothers and sisters were people who did the will of God (see Mk. 3:31-35). Jesus, in spite of the close and intimate union with his holy Mother, separated himself even from her so that no one could mistake his mission to do his Father's will.

Mary was first mentioned in Scripture in St. Paul's letter to the Galatians (4:4-5), which was written around 48 or 50 A.D., some 15 to 17 years after the death, resurrection and ascension of Christ.

The apostle writes, "God sent forth his Son, born of a woman...." Paul does not name her or even mention that she was a virgin.

In Mark (written about 70 A.D.), we first hear of Mary only in that passage already quoted (3:31-35) in which Jesus seems willing to separate himself, for sake of his public mission, from the son-mother relationship. Again, Mary is not named, nor is she called a virgin, in this first mention in a gospel.

This does not mean that her virginity or the virgin birth of Jesus was ever doubted. It means that the sacred writers had other things on their minds. In Galatians Paul was interested in showing that the Son of God, who pre-existed with the Father, had become man, born of "a woman" as all other men are born. Mark's Gospel is concerned with Jesus' total concentration on his mission and his acknowledgement of no law other than the Father's will.

Then we look at Matthew, written around 85 A.D., even though Luke predates Matthew. The writer of Matthew, it is believed, used Mark as a source for his own gospel. In Matthew, we find the sacred writer concentrating on Joseph, Jesus' legal father, through whose home he belongs to the house of David as was prophesied. Because Matthew is primarily concerned with Joseph and the genealogy of Jesus, his mention of Mary is all the more significant. He emphasizes Mary's virginity and he concludes his genealogy this way: "Jacob was the father of Joseph, the husband of Mary, of whom Jesus was born" (1:16). Furthermore, each time Jesus is named in the infancy narrative of Matthew (chapters one and two) he is linked with his mother Mary (see 1:18, 2:11, 13, 14, 20, 21):

In Matthew, Mary's "virginal and supernatural conception is beyond dispute" (Graystone):

"Now this is how the birth of Jesus Christ came about. When his mother Mary was engaged to Joseph, but before they lived together, she was found with child through the power of the Holy Spirit. Joseph her husband, an upright man unwilling to expose her to the law, decided to divorce her quietly. Such was his intention when suddenly the angel of the Lord ap-

peared in a dream and said to him: 'Joseph, son of David, have no fear about taking Mary as your wife. It is by the Holy Spirit that she conceived this child. She is to have a son and you are to name him Jesus because he will save his people from their sins.' All this happened to fulfill what the Lord said through the prophet:

'The virgin shall be with child
and give birth to a son
and they shall call him Emmanuel,'

a name which means 'God is with us''' (Mt. 1:18-23).

Matthew leaves no doubt that Mary is a virgin, that she conceived by the Holy Spirit and that her Son, Jesus, is the Son of God.

In the Gospel of Luke, we find the most popular account of the Nativity of Jesus, complete with Mary, Joseph, the Infant, a stable, animals, shepherds and choirs of angels.

It is vivid, moving and captivating.

The Virgin Birth

Luke was written about 75 A.D., about five years after Mark and ten years before Matthew. The question arises, "If the virgin birth and Mary herself are so important, why aren't they present in the earliest writings, or at least in all four gospels?"

It can be explained this way. The kerygma (basic message of salvation proclaimed by the apostles) centered on the death and resurrection or Jesus. That was the message, as Peter himself proclaimed on the first Pentecost:

"Men of Israel, listen to me! Jesus the Nazorean was a man whom God sent to you with miracles, wonders, and signs as his credentials.... He was delivered up by the set purpose and plan of God; you even made

*use of pagans to crucify and kill him. God freed him
from death's bitter pangs, however, and raised him up
again, for it was impossible that death should keep its
hold on him.... This is the Jesus God has raised up, and
we are his witnesses.... Therefore, let the whole house
of Israel know beyond any doubt that God has made
both Lord and Messiah this Jesus whom you crucified"*
(Acts 2:22-36).

The power of Peter's Spirit-filled preaching, his
proclamation of the Lordship of Jesus and his resurrection from the dead added 3,000 Christians to the
Church that day.

This was the message that captured the imagination and hearts of the disciples and those who heard
them.

As time went on, however, there was a natural desire to know more about this Jesus who came from
Nazareth. Who was he? Who were his parents? I can
imagine the faithful followers of Jesus talking among
themselves until they found someone who could recall
the events surrounding the birth and early life of Jesus.
Mary, herself, must have discussed these events with
the apostles. She was an integral part of the early
Church (see Acts 1:14).

As she, through God's election and a life of prayer,
was deemed worthy to bring Jesus into the world, we
find Mary at prayer with the apostles, helping prepare
them for the birth of the Church which occurred on the
day the Spirit came, the first Christian Pentecost.

It is possible, I personally think probable, that Mary
was sitting with the apostles and other disciples when
the Holy Spirit came on that first Pentecost (see Acts
2:1ff.).

Mary in the Gospel of John

In the Gospel of John, compiled and edited between 90 and 100 A.D., we find two Marian scenes—
at Cana and at Calvary. In John's account, Mary is with
Jesus at the beginning of his public ministry and at its
consummation.

John does not write in a disconnected way. All the
events of his gospel are related to the central theme of
the Incarnation of the Son of God. That Mary is so intimately involved—in Jesus' first miracle and at the
foot of the Cross—tells us that in John's eyes, Mary is
important.

John does not give us another infancy narrative. He
must have been content with those already related in
Matthew and Luke. He does, however, begin with that
moving and holy proclamation that "In the beginning
was the Word, the Word was in God's presence, and the
Word was God.... The Word became flesh and made his
dwelling among us, and we have seen his glory: the
glory of an only Son coming from the Father, filled with
enduring love" (Jn. 1:1-2, 14).

This is John's gift to the Church, a testimony to the
divinity of Jesus, a testimony illuminated by a deep
faith and fed by a desire to counter the Jewish efforts
to discredit both the Church and her founder. In John
we find both a strong belief in the divinity of Jesus and
a near preoccupation with putting the dissenting Jewish leaders in their place.

At Cana, when Mary tells Jesus the hosts are em-
barrassed because they have run out of wine, her Son
addresses her as "woman." Again, this is not a title
given a mother by a loving son, but this is another example of how Jesus is trying his best to let everyone
know his most important relationship is the one he has

with his Father and his most important task is accomplishing the Father's will.

In spite of his response, Mary still trusts that her loving Son will not disappoint her and let the people suffer undue embarrassment. She did not know what Jesus would do. Maybe she thought he'd ask a wealthy man to send for more wine. But, knowing her Son, she told the stewards, "Do whatever he tells you." We all know the story (Jn. 2:1-11). Jesus changed about one hundred gallons of water into the best of wines!

On Calvary, Jesus again calls his mother, "woman." As he hangs on the cross, he tells her to look upon John as her son: "Woman, there is your son." And he says to John, "There is your mother." We are told that, from that day, John took Mary into his own home (see Jn. 19:25-27).

Mother of Christians and of the Church

Graystone, however, holds that "it is evident that the evangelist intends something further, not simply a private gesture, but an act of public and messianic significance." Graystone notes that John was not addressed first, but that Jesus seems to impose motherhood on Mary as he speaks first to her, "Woman, behold your son."

It has long been Catholic understanding that all of Jesus' actions as he hung on the cross had great, and more than personal, significance. On the cross there can be no doubt that he was fully Messiah, Redeemer, Savior. His every thought, breath, act was redemptive and of universal significance. He was without reproach. He did not condemn his enemies. He forgave all. He gave his mother to all.

Catholics, at last reading and studying Scripture, are better able to explain their devotion to Mary to

DO WHATEVER HE TELLS YOU: FINDING JOY IN PLEASING GOD   115

those who depend entirely on Scripture for their inspiration, to those who do not have the blessing of revelation from Tradition.

In being created without sin by God and in having never sinned, Mary is the new Eve. Just as Jesus is the new Adam.

In Jesus and Mary, we see God giving both male and female another chance at being all that humans are supposed to be.

In Jesus and Mary we find anew the call to become holy and to live as children of God.

The Immaculate Conception (Mary's preservation from original sin as she was conceived in her mother's womb) is not for Mary alone. It is a sign of how we are after baptism—completely washed clean, returned to the innocence and purity of Adam and Eve before their fall into sin.

Mary is so important and precious to us.

We love her and honor her—and make no apologies.

For Personal Reflection

Scripture

"Then Mary said: 'My being proclaims the greatness of the Lord, my spirit finds joy in God my savior; for he has looked upon his servant in her lowliness; all ages shall call me blessed'" (Lk. 1:46-48).

Prayer

Lord, I want to be able to say with Mary, "My being proclaims the greatness of the Lord!" Please help me to overcome whatever stands between you and me. Help me to want to do whatever you ask me to do. I love you, Lord, and I want to do your will. Amen.

Examination of Conscience

Honor your father and mother.

You shall not kill.

Mary and Joseph served God by parenting Jesus. Mary gave him life through the Holy Spirit. She and Joseph sustained that life by being good parents. When we love God, we accept the gift of life gratefully and we respect life and protect it—as did Mary and Joseph.

There are many attacks against the sanctity of human life.

Babies are killed in the womb. Elderly parents and grandparents are shunted aside and left to die alone or among strangers. Children and spouses are abused. The weak are oppressed by the strong. Illegal drug traffic, alcoholism and prostitution take a toll on life.

1. How do I respond to these challenges and opportunities?

- Do I honor my parents, aware that through them I am connected to the stream of human life? If they are elderly, do I care for them, visit them, call them, see that they have adequate medical care, food and recreation?

- Do I honor God, the Father of all life, by standing for life from the womb to the tomb? Have I been connected with an abortion, with killing someone on purpose or through carelessness?

- Have I reflected anew on the entire notion of war, peace, the use of conventional and nuclear arms?

- Am I sensitive to the feelings of others, realizing that psychological violence can be just as deadly as physical violence? Do I seek peace instead of argument, a mutually satisfying solution in disagreements rather than victory at any cost?

- Do I have a personal relationship with Mary, the mother of Jesus and my mother as well? Or is she just someone who gets a passing nod around Christmas time?

2. Jesus was at peace because he did the will of the Father and he trusted the Father.

- In facing problems and responsibilities, do I trust the Father or do I still feel ''it's all up to me?''

- What can I do to increase my faith and trust in God?

Decision

To increase my faith and trust in God, and to obey the commandments to revere and protect life, I will

_____

_____

_____

_____

_____

_____

_____ .

Prayer

Lord, I promise to do my best to honor all life, to be open to life, to defend life. I want to love my parents and honor them as you will and as they deserve. I want to develop a holy patience with everyone who demands of me my time, talent and treasure. I want to respond to them as lovingly as you do, as lovingly as I would respond to you if I saw you face-to-face.

Mary, my mother, please pray for me. Intercede, Mary, that I may live the kind of life that Jesus wants me to live. Amen.

For Shared Reflection

Scripture

(After the Ascension of Jesus, the apostles and disciples) "returned to Jerusalem from the mount called Olivet near Jerusalem—a mere Sabbath's journey away. Entering the city, they went to the upstairs room where they were staying: Peter and John and James and Andrew; Philip and Thomas, Bartholomew and Matthew; James son of Alphaeus; Simon, the Zealot party member.... Together they devoted themselves to constant prayer. There were some women in their company, and Mary the mother of Jesus, and his brothers" (Acts 1:12-14).

Prayer

Lord, make us one. Help us to love one another as you love us. If we love, we will wait together for your many comings in our life; we will help one another; we will work together to increase your kingdom through the power of your Spirit. Help us achieve the zeal and trust of the first disciples as they waited and lived for you in the early Church. Amen.

Discussion Starters

1. The apostles and Mary always gathered with the other disciples for prayer, to await the coming of the Spirit, to discern what God wanted them to do.

• In what ways do we imitate the example of Mary and the apostles as a community totally dedicated to prayer and the will of the Lord?

• Do we believe that Jesus still sends the Holy Spirit to teach, guide and strengthen us individually and as a faith community with a mission? Give examples of how our family, small group or parish shows dependence on the Holy Spirit.

2. How can we help others understand the importance of Mary in our lives and help them become more
aware of her powerful intercession?

3. Do we fully appreciate the dignity of human life,
the need to care for the weak and the elderly? As a family, parish or prayer group, what can we do to enhance
respect for life in our society, to reach out to those in need,
comfort the elderly, give good parenting to the young and
wise counsel to our peers?

4. What can we do to promote the general public
health and safety of all of us?

Decision

Here we have a two-part decision.

1. To strengthen our unity in Jesus through the
Holy Spirit, we will _____

_____

_____

_____

_____

_____

_____.

2. To enhance respect for all human life, to promote concern for the elderly and the defenseless, we
will _____

_____

_____

_____

_____

_____

_____

_____.

Prayer

Lord, we have many opportunities to bring the gospel to everyone. Help us to become true children of Mary, Christians who without hesitation embrace your will. Help our parish to become a strong sign of your life and love through our worship and loving service to all in need. We are your people. You are our God. Amen.

Chapter Six

The Church: Mother, Teacher and People of God

"When Jesus came to the neighborhood of Caesarea Philippi, he asked his disciples this question: 'Who do people say that the Son of Man is?' They replied, 'Some say John the Baptizer, others Elijah, still others Jeremiah or one of the prophets.' 'And you,' he said to them, 'who do you say that I am?' 'You are the Messiah,' Simon Peter answered, 'the Son of the living God!' Jesus replied, 'Blest are you, Simon son of Jonah! No mere man has revealed this to you, but my heavenly Father. I for my part declare to you, you are "Rock," and on this rock I will build my church, and the jaws of death shall not prevail against it. I will entrust to you the keys of the kingdom of heaven. Whatever you declare bound on earth shall be bound in heaven; whatever you declare loosed on earth shall be loosed in heaven.' Then he strictly ordered his disciples not to tell anyone that he was the Messiah" (Mt. 16:13-20).

A woman had been away from the Church for twenty years. She had struggled long and hard with guilt. She was divorced and mistakenly believed she was excommunicated—so she never went to church. "Every time I drove by the parish church, I felt an urge to stop by and go in. One day, after a family funeral, I was at home and I asked Jesus to help me. It was almost as though I heard a voice say, 'Go to Mass.'

"It was Sunday morning. I got out of bed, got dressed and went to Mass. A nun spoke during the Mass about all the ministries in the parish. After Mass I went up to her and told her that I had been away for twenty years. She threw her arms around me, gave me a big hug and said, 'Welcome home!' Other parishioners came up to me and hugged me, welcoming me.

"It was the most touching moment of my life. I knew I was home. I love the Church and I love my parish."

This woman's story underscores the power of love and faith in the Christian community. The Church is just that—a community of Christians made one through their faith and love in Jesus and one in their desire to love others as he loves.

I can't emphasize enough the importance of actively living in, for and with the Church as we try to walk more in light and less in darkness.

Not everyone appreciates the importance of the Church, but a careful reading of the New Testament makes it very clear that Jesus founded a community (the Church) to continue his work on earth.

The first time the word "church" ever appears in the Bible is in the above passage, in the Gospel of Matthew written around 85 A.D. (according to the introduction to Matthew in the *New American Bible*).

The Acts of the Apostles, Pauline letters, pastoral letters and Book of Revelation all make many references to the Church, but we find in the gospels only two references which are in Matthew—and they come from the mouth of Christ himself.

It is very important, to deepen our understanding of who we are as Church, to study this passage from Matthew rather closely. There is a lot of information and inspiration here. The setting of the scene is important, as are the people in it. The action of God in Peter's life, the events leading up to his confession of faith, and his selection by Jesus to be the Rock are all very important.

As Jesus approaches this revelation of himself as Messiah, he has already shown his great power—and his openness to the needs of people other than the Hebrews: he has walked on water, confronted the hypocritical Pharisees, healed the daughter of a pagan Canaanite woman (much to the consternation of the disciples), healed other sick people, multiplied the loaves and fish and again warned the people to beware of the Pharisees.

At this point in Matthew, Jesus will soon be moving toward Jerusalem, where he will suffer, die and rise again. He is beginning to feel a sense of urgency in helping his closest disciples recognize who he is, that he is more than the political Messiah everyone expects and desires.

He retires from the Sea of Galilee to Caesarea Philippi, literally, the City of Caesar, where a magnificent temple had been built by Herod the Great. Later, Herod's son, Philip, further beautified it and added his own name to the town.

The city was filled with pagan temples. It is fitting that Jesus should choose such a setting to reveal himself as the Son of the true God. In doing so, Jesus is saying, there is no God but the God of Abraham, Isaac and Jacob.

Also important to this scene is the belief that the Jordan River had its source from springs in that area. The Jordan figured closely with the story of Israel and all of salvation history. Jesus himself was baptized in the Jordan. The Jordan was the river in which Naaman, a pagan, had to bathe in order to be healed of leprosy. The Jordan was a holy river for the Hebrews. If Jesus chose the site of its source to reveal himself as Messiah, he is making a statement to all the Hebrews: I am the source of all life, the fountain of living water, the co-creator with the Father, the Promised One, He Who Is To Come.

First, Jesus asks who people say the "Son of Man" is; then he asks the disciples, "but who do you say that I am?"

It seems he is laying claim to being the Son of Man.

The disciples tell him that some people say he is John the Baptist come back from the dead. John was so great a prophet that it would not have surprised some people had he suddenly reappeared, proclaiming the advent of God's kingdom. Other people believed Jesus to be Elijah: in recognizing him as Elijah the people were saying Jesus was as great as any prophet. Second, if Jesus was Elijah-come-again, then he was the fore-runner of the Messiah, for Malachi proclaims (4:5): "Behold, I will send you Elijah the prophet before the great and terrible day of the Lord."

Some people mistook him for Jeremiah who, it was believed, had taken the ark and the altar of incense out of the temple and hidden them for the purpose of pro-ducing them later so that the glory of God could again return to Israel.

By identifying Jesus with these great prophets, people were truly honoring him and paying him a great compliment—but they did not know truly who he was.

Then Jesus turned to his closest friends, the men to whom he would entrust his mission, and asked them who he was.

"You Are the Messiah"

It was Peter who, inspired by God, finally saw through the mist of incomprehension and proclaimed, "You are the Messiah, the Son of the living God!"

Jesus calls Peter blessed by God. He gives him the keys to the kingdom. The giving of keys was a very important sign of authority to the Hebrews. The keys locked away all that was sacred. Keys protected people from robbery and harm.

Keys do not only lock people out, however. Keys can be used to let people into areas they had not previously entered.

This is what the Father did for Peter. He gave Peter the key to the mystery of faith: the realization that Jesus is the Christ, the Messiah, the Son of God.

That Jesus is Son of God and Messiah is the single great truth at the heart of salvation. In giving the keys to Peter, Jesus demonstrates his unity with the Father's decision to single out Peter. He and the Father share the same authority because they are of one mind and heart.

Peter's keys will not lock God away from people, but will open the doors of heaven so all who believe in Jesus may enter as heirs and children of God.

Peter is given the authority to "bind and loose." That authority also governs who can enter the communion of faith, who cannot and who should be excommunicated from it.

At the end of this passage, Jesus does a curious thing. He tells Peter and the others not to tell anyone that he is the Messiah. Scholars explain that he does this because the disciples themselves do not yet fully understand what it means for him to be Messiah.

In an excellent series of four lessons on Mark produced by the Eternal Word Television Network in Birmingham, Father Eugene LaVerdiere, S.S., says that Mark is concerned with helping his community understand two major things: (1) That Jesus is the Messiah and what it means for him to be Messiah; (2) what it means to be followers of the Messiah. (Write EWTN, Irondale, AL 35210.)

Mark shows that Jesus is Messiah, through a parallel passage to the one we are studying from Matthew. He then shows that to be Messiah means to suffer and die. He wanted his community to understand that they, too, had to suffer and experience death before they could experience the fullness of the kingdom.

The community to whom Mark wrote was filled with gloom and doom. They were the victims of oppression and their land was ravaged by a war waged by Rome. They all thought the end was near. Mark insists, however, even with the words with which he opens his gospel ("Here begins the gospel of Jesus Christ, the Son of God"), that the end is not yet, that the Church is only at its beginning, that all believers, like Jesus, have to take up their crosses and plod forward in faith.

The disciples in Matthew's passage, then, do not yet understand what it means for Jesus to be the Messiah, and Jesus wants them to keep quiet until they do.

Now, then, what does this mean to us today?

A Personal Response to Jesus

First, each of us must be able to respond to that question of questions, "Who do you say that I am?"

Until, with Peter, we can say to Jesus, "You are the Son of God, our Savior," until we personally believe we are each saved by Jesus as well as saved as a people, we cannot claim conversion.

We cannot belong to the Church if we do not believe in Jesus—and without the Church, how could we ever hear about Jesus to be able to believe in him? How could we encounter his power to deliver us from evil?

It is possible for people to go to Church and adhere to externals—to rites, prayers and customs—without ever letting Jesus reveal himself to them personally. In *Way, Truth and Life* (subtitled "Living with Jesus as Personal Savior," Daughters of St. Paul, 1989), I wrote about this personal relationship and how people can develop it. People must first accept Jesus as Lord, then turn away from their own ideas of salvation and happiness to embrace Jesus' way. Finally, people have to surrender their lives and let Jesus live fully in them.

This, of course, is a lifelong process and none of us ever truly achieves total conversion or perfection this side of heaven.

Second, the passage from Matthew also means this: We have legitimate, dependable and clear authority in the Church. Peter and the Apostles—and their successors, the pope and bishops of today—are designated by Christ to lead the Church, to teach and inspire it.

"The jaws of death" (error, sin) will not prevail against the Church.

There can be only one Church. Vatican Council II teaches that all baptized Christians belong to the one Church founded by Jesus, regardless of their denominations. However, not all Christians enjoy full communion in the Church; not all Christians can approach the Eucharist because they do not believe what the Church teaches and do not embrace the papacy, which is a sign and source of unity in the Church.

When we are baptized into the Catholic Church, we are receiving the greatest of gifts. We are incorporated into the Body of Christ and united with and through him to the Father and to all other believers throughout time. We are able to participate in the Eucharist, receive Christ's Body and Blood, become one with him as he offers himself to the Father for all our sins.

There are many churches and many holy people in those churches. There will be many people in heaven besides Catholics, but none can truthfully claim they have the fullness of revelation in their various churches. Jesus founded one Church, not twenty or two thousand. He tells us what is true and does not give us conflicting doctrines. Since so many different churches have conflicting teachings, we know they cannot all be right. We have to find that one Church which Jesus founded and to whom he promised protection against error. Only one Church has been around since apostolic times—and that is the Church which is one, holy, Roman, Catholic and apostolic.

On July 14, 1989, Oprah Winfrey's popular talk show featured a black priest from the Archdiocese of Washington, D.C. who has set up his own church. It seems the priest doesn't believe the Catholic Church has done enough for Blacks in general and for black Catholics in particular. He may be right, but setting up your own congregation against the direct orders of your bishop is no way to help the Church grow stronger.

Racism, whether white or black, is still racism. The Catholic Church does not exclude anyone. Doors are open to all. Separating a group from the whole body because of a problem does not solve the problem or heal relationships.

I have never seen a better example of why we need clear, objective norms in deciding what is and is not acceptable in the Church, and what is and is not Catholic.

The Church is God's invention, not ours. Jesus founded the Church to continue his mission of healing, teaching, forgiving, sanctifying and loving. No one but Jesus and those to whom he gave special powers can finally decide what is and is not proper Catholic teaching and discipline.

The controversy surrounding this new "church" established by the black priest, as well as all other controversies, tend to distort the real image of the Church. In dialogue and arguments, we seem most often to end up talking about "them and us." "Them" is the institution, and "us" is everyone who feels persecuted, ignored or in some way hurt by the institution.

What we often disparagingly call the "institution," as separate from the "real Church," is made up of people like you and me, people with strengths and weaknesses, with good days and bad days, with hopes and disappointments, with insights and doubts. People who represent the institution are responsible for defending it, when necessary, and their job is not a popular one. In fact, I have spoken with bishops and priests who, caught in the midst of controversy, suffered great sorrow that the people they wanted most to help were estranged from them by prejudiced notions of the "institution."

Regardless of the subject of the controversy—abortion, race relations, birth control, homosexuality, women's rights—we must all remember two things:

1. If we are Catholic, we are part of the institution; we have an obligation to make the Church stronger, and,

2. The Church is more than the institution, but its institutional functions are crucial to its operations and survival. We need an organization to order and regulate our community affairs or we will not long have a Church.

Jesus gave his apostles authority to govern, guide and sanctify his Church. In spite of many difficulties and even scandals over the years, Jesus has made good his promise to remain with his Church and to defend it against the gates of hell.

Back to Our Roots

Parish or universal Church, we have to go back to our roots to understand who we are as the people Jesus has chosen as his own. However, there is something very romantic about the early Church and, if we are not careful, we will so romanticize those first years that we will not be able to identify the present with the past.

There was indeed power and might and miracles in the early Church—but there was persecution, dissention and misunderstanding as well. There were many personal and institutional problems in the early Church. We should not be surprised that we find ourselves in the same dilemma today.

You may want to read the Acts of the Apostles which is, in fact, the first history of the Church; next, read your diocesan newspaper and notice the similarities between the early Church and the modern Church.

As you read Acts you will find the selection of Matthias to replace the traitor Judas, the ordination of seven deacons to help solve a major social problem in the infant Church—tensions between the Greek and Jewish Christians (Acts 6). You will find the hypocrisy of people who pretend to be faithful to the Church's call to live in common but horde their personal treasures. There are examples of the abuse of power, of shaky faith, of people willing to suffer and die for the Name, examples of misunderstanding and serious contention between leaders in the Church. You will see that Paul was quite angry with the Jewish Christians who kept insisting on circumcision for gentile Christians; Paul, Barnabas and Mark have such a fight that Paul leaves their company.

In the early Church you will find legalism as well as charism, and the tensions that always result between the status quo and the call to ever deeper conversion.

Don't we have the same situation today throughout the world? There are problems between Protestants and Catholics in Ireland (although the problem is more political and economic than religious). There are difficulties right here in America as Hispanics grow in number and Blacks make a bid for a higher profile. We have had our share of scandals of all kinds—including racism, sexism, triumphalism.

The apostles had theological problems as well. One of the greatest tensions was between "the Law" and the gospel which called all people to salvation through faith in Christ and not through the Law.

In our present day, we have many such conflicts. There is great controversy surrounding the magisterium's teachings on remarriage after divorce, abortion, the ordination of women, celibacy and human sexuality.

Respond in Love, Good Conscience

What saddens me is not the controversy so much as disregard for the Lord's command that we love one another. If the greatest of virtues is love, it is a grave sin not to love.

Perhaps Christians need to think more about how they fail to love others. It is easy to consider the usual sins of "the flesh" or of "the world." But the sin of "the heart," to fail to love, comes from within and is rooted in pride. It is hard to admit such sin—but until we do, there is no way in which the Lord can deliver us from that evil.

The fundamental question for each of us is this: "Given my faith in Jesus Christ, how do I respond to problems in the Church and people who, for me, are a problem?"

I would suggest several things to help us respond in love and in good conscience.

1. *Know what the Church really teaches, and why.* One of the greatest wrongs committed against the Church by the secular media and even by Catholic dissenters who know better—is quoting out of context. When the Holy Father issued his great document, *On the Role of the Family in the Modern World,* all the secular press generally reported was that he had affirmed the Church's teachings against divorce and artificial birth control.

What a terrible offense against truth!

Don't trust the secular media to help you understand the fundamental values upon which the magisterium bases its teachings. In fact, don't rely solely on your diocesan paper because, if it is like most of the Catholic papers, it simply does not have the room, time, budget and personnel to present such subjects in sufficient depth.

To understand better what the pope, for example, has to say about human sexuality and family life, we need to read the pope. It's that simple.

There is a book that gives a good explanation of Pope John Paul II's underlying philosophy to all his teachings on human life, sexuality, work and relationships. It is published by Image Books and called, *Covenant of Love.*

You may also want to read the encyclicals, the pastoral letters, the documents published by the Vatican and various conferences of bishops. To acquire a copy of a given document, you may write *Origins,* c/o Catholic News Service, 3211 4th St. NE, Washington, DC, 20017-1194.

2. *Please be honest.* Several years ago, an evangelical magazine published a story about a former Catholic priest. He had been a well known priest. The cover portrayed him with his wife and children. He had not

been laicized. The article, an interview with the ex-priest, in part cast a bad light on the Church, blaming the Church for not understanding that this man had a right to marry.

The article said that the priest had gone to his superior *two weeks before he got married* to seek permission to marry—and, as I recall, the priest felt he had not been treated fairly because he was not given permission to marry. I told the publisher the article was unfair to the Roman Catholic Church. He told me that the former priest had read and approved the article before it was published.

He truly did not understand that the priest had misrepresented the Church. I explained that it would take a rather irresponsible Church to excuse a man from a solemn vow on two weeks' notice! The priest took a solemn vow before God and the Church to live as a celibate for the sake of the kingdom. How could the Church ignore that vow or let him treat it casually?

People who disagree with the Church, Catholics and others as well, should always be honest. Don't lie about what the Church says and does.

Don't make smug remarks that dismiss out of hand the legitimate authority of the magisterium. Such an attitude fosters untruth and is far from responsible or charitable.

At the same time, the teachers in the Church have an obligation to treat all dissenters with respect and take their ideas seriously, to consider them and respond either favorably or unfavorably to them.

3. *Don't practice character assassination.* There is no room in the Church for slander. It is not Christian to hurt another person's good name. Whenever someone, arguing either for or against the official Church position, stoops to name-calling, run in the opposite

direction. It does no good to make fun of "curial min-ions" or to label everyone who disagrees with Rome a "heretic."

If we have to resort to name-calling to win an argument or to win people over to our cause, we do not have an argument to begin with!

4. *Have a faithful attitude.* A person who loves God and the truth will have a faithful attitude—will treasure communion and unity in the Church above all his or her own ideas.

Father Charles Curran comes to mind. Father Curran is not excommunicated. He can function as a priest. He has had his license to teach Catholic theology in Catholic University removed by Rome. I have spoken with many people who studied under him. They all speak highly of him. But Rome was not satisfied that what he was teaching as Catholic doctrine was indeed truly Catholic doctrine.

History will finally tell whether any or all of his controversial positions finally had any merit.

I think Father Curran made a mistake. His positions were well known. He had had much publicity, had written books and given lectures. If he had chosen to be silent, his positions would still have remained well known—and his witness of obedience to the magisterium would have added strength to his arguments.

It seems he could not, in conscience, obey Rome's directive to refrain from certain of his teachings. What about his vow of obedience? Isn't that a question of conscience as well?

It seems to me that Father Curran's insistence in maintaining his public dissent forced the magisterium to take decisive action against him.

At the same time, Church authority must never become heavy-handed for the sake of the status quo. While there is a large difference between the relationship of Catholic theologians with the magisterium and the relationship of the early Church with the Jewish leaders, one New Testament passage offers a caution to today's religious authorities.

The famous Rabbi Gamaliel told the Sanhedrin when that Jewish court was considering what to do with Christians: "My advice is that you have nothing to do with these men. Let them alone. If their purpose or activity is human in its origins, it will destroy itself. If, on the other hand, it comes from God, you will not be able to destroy them without fighting God himself" (Acts 5:38b-39).

One of the great burdens of the magisterium is to discern the difference between prophets and fools. Sometimes, we have to admit, we have fools on either or both sides of the debate. We also have to admit that we sometimes have silenced, and undoubtedly will sometimes silence in the future, saints who were speaking for God.

Faithful in Ambiguity

That risk comes with the territory. Our task is to remain as faithful in ambiguity and doubt as we are in what is clearly inspirational and uncontested in faith. We have to believe that Jesus' promise to preserve us from error works in ambiguity as well as in certainty.

Part of the problem with Catholic Christians today is their desire for instant solutions. The Church is still growing. There are always new problems which demand answers, but quick answers are not always possible. We are facing many new challenges. The technological explosion, the conquest of space, nuclear power and nuclear wastes, genetic manipulation, surrogate motherhood, the imbalance of wealth and power, the threat of global annihilation, massive famines and new epidemics of deadly diseases such as AIDS, the

Third World and its demands for justice and independence—these new challenges force the Church to restudy its formulation of doctrine. Truth does not change, but the depth in which we understand truth and the manner in which we express it do change.

We could go on, but the point is made. The Church today, as in the early days, has failures and successes, heroes and cads, problems and uncertainties, God's grace and the human inability to respond constantly and without frequent hesitation to that grace.

It is a great mystery discovered by Paul that God's grace is enough for us, that "in weakness power reaches perfection" (2 Cor. 13:9).

We will become a stronger Church when we realize that God works best when we admit we are helpless. As a Church we must experience ongoing conversion and come to Eucharist with the understanding that alone we are too weak to change, that only God, in his great goodness and power, can help us become what we are supposed to be.

In Vatican Council II, the Lord called us to a deep, interior and spiritual renewal. We got sidetracked with external changes. The call of God persists and insists: repent and be saved; repent and let me renew you in my Spirit.

After our next reflection, we will consider how we repent as Church.

For Personal Reflection

Scripture

"...Jesus [the Messiah] started to indicate to his disciples that he must go to Jerusalem and suffer greatly there at the hands of the elders, the chief priests, and the scribes, and to be put to death, and raised up on the third day. At this, Peter took him aside and began to remonstrate with him. 'May you be spared, Master! God forbid that any such thing ever happen to you!' Jesus turned on Peter and said, 'Get out of my sight, you Satan! You are trying to make me trip and fall. You are not judging by God's standards but by man's.'

"Jesus then said to his disciples: 'If a man wishes to come after me, he must deny his very self, take up his cross, and begin to follow in my footsteps. Whoever would save his life will lose it, but whoever loses his life for my sake will find it'" (see Mt. 16:21-25).

Prayer

Jesus, it is hard to love in the midst of tensions, hard to believe, sometimes, that you really are with the Church. I need to learn to love more completely and unconditionally. When I must disagree with people, help me to respond in charity rather than react self-righteously and in anger. Amen.

Examination of Conscience

You shall not bear dishonest witness against your neighbor.

You shall not desire your neighbor's goods.

1. With all the pressures put on people to get and hold their jobs, there is always the temptation to secure one's position at the expense of others, to put one's trust in material possessions.

- Am I a "worry wart?" Am I so anxious about life that I cannot enjoy it or that I make life miserable for others?

- Have I gossiped or even told lies about others in order to get ahead?

2. There are specific tensions, problems and opportunities in our Church today.

- Am I looking for Jesus in all situations, trying to discern what he wants of me?

- Have I made the kind of commitment to Christ that enables me to "ride" with the tensions, remain faithful to his Word, and loving to those with whom I disagree?

3. Jesus asks me, today: "And you. Who do you say I am?"

- Do I firmly believe Jesus is the Son of God, the Messiah, the Savior of the world, my own personal Lord and Savior?

- Am I so in love with Jesus that I want to share him with others?

Decision

To discipline myself to respond in love to others, especially to those who disagree with me, I will

_____

_____

_____

_____

_____

_____

_____.

Prayer

Jesus, I accept you as my Lord and Savior. I give myself to you. I ask you to forgive me my sins and to deliver me from all evil. I want to serve you, Jesus, now and always. Fill me with a sense of your presence. Teach me to love the Father. Give me true wisdom—the ability to want what you want, Lord.

Jesus, through your Spirit give me a deep understanding of scripture and help me to live it daily and to share it with others. Help me to become so close to you that with St. Paul, I can say, "The life I live now is not my own; Christ is living in me." Amen.

For Shared Reflection

Scripture
    "You, however, are a 'chosen race, a royal priest-
hood, a holy nation, a people he claims for his own to
proclaim the glorious works' of the One who called you
from darkness into his marvelous light. Once you were
no people, but now you are God's people; once there
was no mercy for you, but now you have found mercy"
(see 1 Pt. 2:9-10).

Prayer
    Jesus, as we share your love during this time
together, please open our minds and hearts to grasp
better the meaning of being your Church, your people.
Amen.

Discussion Starters
    1. An American priest has said, "The problem is
that most Catholics sitting in Church on Sunday have
been sacramentalized but not evangelized."

• What do you think he meant by that statement?

• Do you agree or disagree with the statement?

• Do Catholics, generally speaking, know Jesus as
  personal Lord and Savior—and do they readily share
  their faith in him?

    2. Cardinal Jozef Ratzinger, prefect of the Congre-
gation for the Doctrine of the Faith in Rome, once said
that there is a danger that Catholics in the United States
forget that Jesus is divine as well as human. He said,
too, that in America there is a great wave of materialism which weakens the faith of Catholics.

• Is there any evidence that Catholics are forgetting
  that Jesus is both divine and human? Are we affected
  by materialism?

- Do we as a parish fall victim to consumerism and materialism—and if so, how?

- What can we do in our own family, prayer group or parish to help us remember that Jesus is both God and man?

3. The Second Vatican Council and Pope John Paul II have urged the laity to become effective witnesses to Jesus Christ in the world, to open their homes to the homeless, to practice in Jesus' name the virtue of hospitality among the disenfranchised and abused.

- How can our parish help people develop an awareness of their baptismal obligation to minister to others?

- How can we, as a parish, respond more effectively to the call to spread the news about God's mercy and invite others into the Church?

Decision

As a community of faith, to promote lay participation in spreading the gospel in our parish and local community, we agree to _____

_____

_____

_____

_____

_____

_____

_____

_____.

Prayer

Fill us with your Spirit, Lord. Let every man, woman and child in our parish be in love with you and eager to do what you want your people to do.

Help us to worship with great love and joy, for you deserve the best we can give in all things. We want visitors to our parish to be inspired to seek a deeper relationship with you.

Let us be, Lord, the apple of your eye. Amen.

Chapter Seven

The Repentant Church

(Peter, in his first sermon on Pentecost) "kept urging, 'Save yourselves from this generation which has gone astray.' Those who accepted his message were baptized; some three thousand were added that day.

"They devoted themselves to the apostles' instruction and the communal life, to the breaking of bread and the prayers. A reverent fear overtook them all, for many wonders and signs were performed by the apostles. Those who believed shared all things in common; they would sell their property and goods, dividing everything on the basis of each one's need. They went to the temple area together every day, while in their homes they broke bread. With exultant and sincere hearts they took their meals in common, praising God and winning the approval of all the people. Day by day the Lord added to their number those who were being saved" (Acts 2:40-47).

The Church is not perfect. Sometimes people let the sins of others, especially those of priests and bishops, keep them from practicing their faith. That's like saying, I will never eat in this restaurant because the owner spilled a glass of water.

I love the Catholic Church. I need the Catholic Church. If I hope to overcome the darkness and sin in my life, I need the Catholic Church, with all her warts and blemishes, with all her saints and sinners.

The Church is God's gift to us, the way in which he continues to live among us, in us, for us. It is in the Church that we discover the fullness of what God wants to say to us and do for us.

Yes, we are the Church, sinners that we are—and it is in us that Jesus reveals himself, through us that the world comes to know him. I take great joy in being a Christian, but my heart is filled with gratitude that God chose me to be also a Catholic.

One day, someone asked me, "Are you a Catholic or a Christian?"

I was young at that time, had just come back to the Church after our son was saved from death through the intercession of Mary. There was, however, a certainty in me that let me answer, "To be Catholic is to be fully Christian."

When a Catholic embraces what the Church teaches, he or she is deeply in love with Jesus and committed to his will.

Only the Roman Catholic Church can trace itself back, through the laying on of hands, to Peter and the other apostles who, ordained by Jesus himself, were the Fathers of the Church.

A Repenting Church

We would be foolish, however, to deny that in our Church we have had many scandals and periods in which certain popes, bishops and faithful did not honor God.

The Crusades were not as spiritually pure as people wanted to believe; the Spanish Inquisition, in spite of its purpose of protecting truth, was responsible for unspeakable crimes against justice; one pope silenced Galileo, under threat of torture, because the astronomer correctly claimed that the earth revolved around the sun; in mission lands, some missionaries abused people and forced their own cultures upon the natives. We could go on, but not without running the risk of distorting the true image or our Church, which for nearly two thousand years has preached the gospel, helped the poor, healed the sick, protected the weak and challenged all peoples to live in harmony and peace, to practice justice and to live as sacred creations of God.

The Church has already "repented" for the Crusades and the Spanish Inquisition. We have admitted our fault and turned to better ways. The Church has already repented of the activities of mistaken missionaries. Today, the Church is one of the greatest champions for preserving what is good in all cultures.

Pope John Paul II in all his travels has shown how the Church should embrace all peoples in all cultures. He has worn the headdress of Native American chiefs and eaten the native foods of Africans, Asians, Orientals, Hispanics, Americans and Eskimos. In his love for all peoples, the Holy Father has remained faithful to God, the Church and truth.

The U.S. bishops have shown courageous faith in addressing some of the most pressing issues facing the world today—poverty, war and peace. The bishops' collective voice is saying, "Faith in Jesus Christ means love and justice for all people. Faith in Jesus Christ means that we embrace the mission of Jesus to heal and comfort, to enable and liberate, as well as to preach truth and lead people into eternal life.''

The Catholic laity, generally speaking, will help feed the hungry and send people to the missions, but they do not feel comfortable in trying to bring their friends, neighbors, co-workers and even their relatives to Jesus and into the Church. I have treated this topic in greater detail in *Miracle in the Marketplace* (Resurrection Press, Williston Park, N.Y., 1990). Here, I want to reflect on faith, justice and truth. This may help readers who want to understand better their pursuit of holiness and thus make them more comfortable in sharing their faith.

Clarifying the Power of Faith

Justice has become an important issue in defining what it means to be and live as a Catholic. There is great emphasis on the ''balance of wealth'' and ''enabling'' individual poor people and poor nations to overcome their own problems. The Church is becoming more and more concerned with nuclear war, ecology and the interdependence of nations.

This broad and urgent emphasis on such global and seemingly, to some, secular issues, along with disagreements in the Church about theology and personal moral issues, may well invite confusion about precisely what Catholics are supposed to believe and share with others.

Let's look briefly at faith, truth and justice.

Faith. Faith is a gift we receive at Baptism, but it is not a lifeless commodity, such as a precious diamond. Faith is a living reality. The gift of faith is a share in the very mind, heart and life of God. Through faith, Christ lives in us, he and the Father make their home in us, the Holy Spirit fills us with the life, love and power of God.

Faith is not a deposit of truth. Faith enables us to embrace truth—and more, it impels us to share truth with others.

Faith can transform the world.

Too many Catholics seem to forget that when they receive God's gifts, they have to give them away, not hoard them, in order to keep them. These Catholics have not been taught that they have a responsibility to shout the gospel from the rooftops to attract people into the kingdom.

We Catholics must learn to live as zealous missionaries in our own homes, neighborhoods and marketplace. We must learn to love with selfless abandon.

In 1988, a Florida priest led a group of teenagers on a three-week mission to a very impoverished diocese in the Dominican Republic. One day, the priest and three or four of the American teenagers spent several hours walking down a mountain. They had no water and were very thirsty. A young native boy was with them.

When they finally reached a village at the foot of the mountain, the priest bought soft drinks for himself, all the U.S. teenagers and the young native boy.

The Americans all downed their drinks immediately, but the native boy ran outside, called all his friends together and shared his drink with all of them.

The young boy loved his friends with a selfless abandon. He loved so much he was willing to share the treasure of a rare, cold soft drink.

Sometimes we are slow in learning what being Christian means. Even the disciples who lived and traveled with Jesus often missed the boat when they had to respond to specific challenges. Jesus taught them over and over again what he expected of them—and through the gospel, he teaches us as well.

The disciples of Jesus were at first slow to share what they had (Mark 6:34ff.). At the end of a long day of preaching, five thousand men, plus women and children, were tired and hungry. The disciples suggested that Jesus send them away so they could go to neighboring villages to find something to eat.

Jesus said, "You give them something to eat."

The disciples were shocked. "It would cost two hundred days wages to feed this crowd! Even if we had it, that's asking too much, but we don't have that much!"

Jesus, ever patient, asked, "How many loaves have you?"

They replied, "Five loaves and two fish."

Jesus had the people sit on *the green grass* in *groups or parties.*

Mark goes on to say:

"Then, taking the five loaves and the two fish, Jesus raised his eyes to heaven, pronounced a blessing, broke the loaves, and gave them to the disciples to distribute. He divided the two fish among all of them and they ate until they had their fill. They gathered up enough leftovers to fill twelve baskets, besides what remained of the fish. Those who had eaten numbered five thousand men " (Mk. 6:41-44).

This gospel passage is very important to us as we try to discover how we need to repent as Church.

1. Mark uses imagery which would have appealed immediately to his Jewish audience. The five thousand people are in a desert, but Mark says they are invited to sit on green grass and when there is no food around, the Lord prepares for them a big meal.

In Mark's account, we can easily hear the echoes of Psalm 23 which was familiar to all of Mark's audience: "The Lord is my shepherd; I shall not want. In *verdant pastures* he gives me repose.... You *spread a table* before me...."

Mark is recounting Jesus' miracle in a way that will help remind his community, mostly people familiar with the Hebrew scriptures, that Jesus is the Lord, the Son of God, the promised one.

As Church, we often need to repent of apathy or of taking Jesus for granted.

2. The passage says that Jesus told the multitude to sit down in *groups and parties*. In Luke (9:14), we see that Jesus wanted the multitude to sit down in "groups of 50 or so." In our present day, there has been a lot of emphasis on small communities within the parish, particularly through the RENEW program. Marriage Encounter and Cursillo encourage people to meet in small groups.

While there is but one faith, people need to share that faith intimately with a select group of friends who become prayer partners and helpers in living the Christian life. Many Catholics need to repent of isolating themselves from the rest of the faith community.

3. Perhaps most important of all is the fact that Jesus told the disciples, *"You give them something to eat."*

The disciples balked: "But we don't have enough money or enough food to feed all these people!"

Does that ever sound familiar!

Jesus tells us: "Go and make disciples of all nations. Preach my word. Share your faith."

Like the disciples we respond, "Oh, Jesus, I don't have enough faith. I don't know the Bible. I don't know theology. I'm too shy."

This story from Mark tells us that if we give Jesus the little we have, he will multiply it and make it enough to achieve what he wants achieved. A dear friend has said that "living in faith is like standing with one foot on a banana peeling and the other high in the air." If we don't step out in faith, Jesus cannot work in our lives.

We must give what little we have. We must trust that Jesus will live up to his promise: "...do not worry beforehand about what to say. In that hour, say what you are inspired to say. It will not be yourselves speaking, but the Holy Spirit" (Mk. 13:11b). Jesus was trying to tell the disciples they would face persecution and must trust the Spirit to put the right words in their mouths. Surely, the Spirit will do the same when we trust God enough to try to share our faith with those who need to know how much God loves them.

We must be as open to the Spirit as was Philip, the deacon, who converted the Ethiopian. Philip was minding his own business when an angel told him to take a desert road from Jerusalem to Gaza. He obeyed immediately and came upon the Ethiopian eunuch who was reading Isaiah. Philip struck up a conversation with the official, who incidentally was in charge of the entire treasury of Ethiopia. The man was so inspired by Philip's faith that he requested immediate baptism.

The Spirit put the words in Philip's mouth and he will put the right words in our mouths as well—if only we trust enough to take that first step.

In Mark's account of the multiplication of the loaves and fish, there is still more to learn. After everyone had eaten—five thousand men plus women and children—they gathered up "enough leftovers to fill twelves baskets, besides what remained of the fish." Jesus did not simply multiply the disciples' gifts to meet the immediate need. He provided abundantly. Now everyone had something to share!

To be a good Catholic Christian, we cannot be content only with receiving.

A Deeper Look into Faith

Let's look a little deeper into faith.

The sacred writer of Hebrews tells us (11:1): "Faith is confident assurance concerning what we hope for, and conviction about things we do not see."

Through faith, we are sure that we are saved and will be with one another and God forever in heaven. Through faith, we know that we are forgiven and that God can and does make a difference in our lives here and now. Through faith, we know that we can accomplish things, with God's generous and loving help, that are far beyond our normal capabilities.

What Hebrews says of Abraham and his wife, Sarah, is of utmost importance to us as we speak of a Church repenting for lack of faith.

"By faith Abraham obeyed when he was called, and went forth to the place he was to receive as a heritage; he went forth, moreover, not knowing where he was going. By faith he sojourned in the promised land as in a foreign country, dwelling in tents with Isaac and Jacob, heirs of the same promise; for he was looking forward to the city with foundations, whose designer and maker is God. By faith Sarah received power to conceive though she was past the age, for she thought that the One who had made the promise was worthy of trust. As a result of this faith, there came forth from one man, who was himself as good as dead, descendants as numerous as the stars in the sky and the sands of the seashore" (Heb. 11:8-12).

Today, we often hear complaints about this or that person, "He doesn't know what he's doing." That's okay, actually, if he is doing God's will!

Abraham didn't know where he was going, and when he got there, in the land God promised him, he did not have a permanent residence, a palace or even a permanent mud hut. He lived in tents, a nomad, moving from place to place. Abraham had been a very wealthy person back where he came from. He left it all to answer the call from God. He looked forward to another place, to the fulfillment of what God promised, even though he likely didn't understand what, precisely, God had promised. He probably felt what we all feel when, at last, we have achieved a long-sought goal: a certain empty disappointment, a certainty that we have not yet achieved "what we hope for."

Abraham and Sarah trusted God, had faith in God. Because they did, and because of Jesus who came from the root of Abraham, we gentiles can call ourselves children of Abraham, children of the Most High God.

Jesus told us that if we "had faith the size of a mustard seed" we could accomplish great things (Mt. 17:20).

He promised us, "You will receive all that you pray for, provided you have faith" (Mt. 21:22).

Jesus forgave the sins of a paralytic and then healed the man because he was moved by the faith of his friends who lowered him through the roof of a house in which Jesus sat teaching (Mk. 2:5).

He told the blind Bartimaeus, "Be on your way. Your faith has healed you" (Mk. 10:52).

When a woman suffering from hemorrhage for a dozen years came up behind Jesus and, in faith, touched the hem of his garment, Jesus felt power leave him. He turned, found the woman and said to her, "Daughter, it is your faith that has cured you. Now go in peace" (see Lk. 8:43-48).

Faith is alive, has power and produces change in oneself and in the world. Is our faith truly alive in the Church today? Do we need to discover again the power of true faith?

Truth. In the movie, "Absence of Malice," Sally Field plays a reporter, Megan, who learned a valuable lesson. She reported facts as she discovered them and got a whole lot of people in trouble, including Gallagher, played by Paul Newman. She fell in love with Gallagher, whom her stories reported as under investigation. She became sexually involved with him. At the end of the movie, she was being interviewed by another reporter who asked about her relationship with Gallagher. Megan responded, after some painful thought, "Just say we were involved."

The other reporter said reflectively, "That's true, isn't it?"

Megan responded, "It's a fact, but not the truth."

There was more to the involvement, for Megan, than implied in the simple statement, "Just say we were involved."

She had grown to love Gallagher, but serious tensions had grown between them because of Gallagher's pride and her callous approach to news reporting.

It was a fact that they were "involved," but that fact fell far short of representing their total relationship, its complexity, and the dashed hopes Megan was now experiencing.

It would be the same if a loving and happily married couple stood up before everybody and said, "We have a sexual relationship." They would be stating a true fact, but their public admission would be far from communicating the truth of their relationship.

For most of us, borrowing the definition from ancient Greek philosophers, something is true when it reveals itself, when the mind can grasp what it is.

In the Bible, however, truth is what we learn from an encounter with God. In the Old Testament, truth meant being faithful to God's covenant and keeping the Law. For us, the people of the New Testament, truth is centered and revealed in Jesus Christ.

It's easy to see how "the world" and the Church are on a collision course. Without benefit of revelation, the world says that it is wrong to steal because stealing undermines the peace and security of society—and also because it violates the victim's rights.

For Christians, however, stealing is wrong for the additional reason that the crime violates the command to love. Stealing is a direct affront to God because it hurts someone he identifies with himself (see Mt. 25:31-40—what we do to the least of Christ's brothers and sisters, we do to him).

Society cannot command us to love. It can command us only not to hurt one another. Only God can command us to love, because only he can give us the power to love.

For us, truth is God's revelation. That's why, for Paul, the law was of no consequence after he saw Jesus face-to-face. Paul saw love incarnate, the greatest motivating power of all, and knew that law, as an external rule, could never measure up to the intimate, demanding, enabling and transforming power of the living Jesus, who comes with his Father and Spirit to live in us in love.

With this in mind, we can ask the question, "Do some people disbelieve certain teachings of the magisterium because they have not looked as deeply into the heart of God as have the teachers of the Church over these two thousand years?"

It is hard to deal with truth without hurting people. There are many people who say they are convinced, in conscience, that the magisterium is wrong in its teaching against artificial birth control.

They insist that the Church (meaning the majority of the people of God) approves of artificial birth control. Many Catholics do disagree with the Holy Father on this point, and still go to communion, consider themselves good Catholics and in fact do a lot of good, in love, for many other people.

However, because I am generous with my time in working for the Church does not make my stinginess with money a virtue.

The dissenters do not see artificial contraception, in itself, as sinful. They are convinced, they say, that since this teaching against artificial birth control has never been declared *ex cathedra*, people can, after informing their consciences, legitimately disagree with the Pope.

In Pope Paul VI's *Humanae Vitae* issued in 1968, he states in paragraphs 11 and 12 that the magisterium has consistently upheld that artificial birth control is immoral. He states that "the conjugal act, while most closely uniting husband and wife, capacitates them for the generation of new lives, according to laws inscribed in the very being of man and of woman. By safeguarding both these essential aspects, the unitive and the procreative, the conjugal act preserves in its fullness the sense of true mutual love and its ordination towards man's most high calling to parenthood. We believe that the men of our day are particularly capable of seizing the deeply reasonable and human character of this fundamental principle."

The present Holy Father's position is clearly based on that tradition and on what, through his own reflections under the inspiration of the Holy Spirit, he understands to be God's revelation of himself and his will in both Scripture and Tradition. His understanding of human nature is rooted in a concept that human beings are integrally both body and spirit.

Like St. Paul in his letter to the Corinthians, Pope John Paul II is insisting that the body is sacred, not unimportant and inconsequential, that the body, like the spirit, must be subject to God. Among the Greeks, the body was indeed inconsequential. Only the spirit or the soul mattered. Since the body was unimportant, it could be abused by severe asceticism at one extreme and pampered by indulgence at the other extreme—without any spiritual consequence.

That is not the Christian understanding of the human person. Going all the way back to Creation, the magisterium holds that human beings were created in the image of God, without sin, innocent, and that all their desires, appetites and powers were in perfect harmony with the will of God.

A person enjoyed food, but had control over his appetite and did not overindulge. A person had sexual desires, but these desires did not control the person. I find it strange that people who justify denying taste buds for sake of physical health and self-discipline cannot understand denying genital pleasure for the sake of physical health and social as well as self-discipline.

The sin of Adam and Eve destroyed the balance of powers in the human person. Christ came to redeem and to heal. We are called to live in Christ, to try to regain that integrity of mind, body and spirit with which we were created. We will never be fully restored to that perfection until we live in eternity with Jesus, but failure to achieve the goal is no reason to change the goal.

Any moral question—sexual, societal, familial, political or economical—is rooted in that basic truth that we are created in the image of God and are called to perfection. Perfection means more than avoidance of sin; it means regaining the balance of powers we had in Eden before the Fall. It is true we can never be perfect this side of heaven. That's why Jesus came, to make up the difference. We cannot, however, stop trying.

The moment we stop trying, we deny truth. When we try to ignore who we were "in the beginning," we make it impossible to become who we must become before "the end."

Justice. "If you want peace, work for justice." This is perhaps one of the most often quoted sayings of Pope Paul VI. It has fueled sermons and newspaper articles for many years.

There can no peace among nations or even in families if people are not treated justly.

Happily, there is great concern for justice in our Church today. In the United States, Catholics are addressing such contemporary problems as the rights of women, the poor and the oppressed. We are concerned with Blacks, Hispanics and other minorities. As a nation, we are still working to help people throughout the world attain freedom and democratic forms of government.

The danger is that we approach justice only from a legalistic point of view. We may seek to change laws and customs, even attitudes, without fulfilling the full mandate of the gospel to convert hearts.

It is conceivable that we could change the plight of Blacks, for example, and ignore what is happening to women, Hispanics and Asians. Such would be far from the New Testament sense of what justice is all about.

Just as peace is more than the absence of war, justice is more than absence of prejudice and oppression. Justice, it seems to me, is more than a realized goal of fair and equal treatment and opportunity for everyone. Part and parcel of justice is the active pursuit of, and the energy expended toward achieving, the positive good and growth of all people.

In the Old Testament, justice was summed up in the Jewish conviction that God would not lie. He promised reward and he promised punishment and he kept those promises for people who, respectively, obeyed or disobeyed his commandments.

In the New Testament, we find Jesus purifying the Jewish concept of justice. Jesus is concerned primarily not with social injustices but with empty religious formalism. He is angered by the lack of faith among the Pharisees and Sadduces, by their hypocrisy.

He has come to fulfill the law, to help people discover the very will and heart of the God who gave them the law. He wants people to experience such deep conversion that they are led by the Spirit to regard God as their personal, loving and intimate Father, to become transformed by faith into loyal sons and daughters of God (see Mt. 5:17-48; 6:1-18). Jesus gives the law new and deeper meaning when he calls people to imitate God in their pursuit of peace, justice, purity, meekness, constancy of faith (see Mt. 5:1ff.).

St. Paul, for his part, develops the theme of justice in terms of response to the saving power of God. God still rewards and punishes, but we are "justified" only through faith in Christ Jesus and not through the Law. For Paul, the Law had authority and heart only because it came from God. Jesus is God incarnate, and response to him in love automatically brings the believer into the will of God. So the Law, and focusing faith in it, becomes a distraction from the call to fulfill God's will through intimate union with him in Christ.

Paul's early teachings on justice tend to focus on the end times, on deliverance from oppression and sin. People will be saved. As his ministry of preaching and writing continues, however, Paul discovers that justice is a here and now reality, that in Christ we are made clean and presentable to the Father. Justice is "a divine grace (which looks to the future end times for fulfillment) but really and presently anticipated in the Christian life. Paul (says) that the justice of God comes down from heaven and that it comes to transform (humankind). It is a blessing belonging essentially to God, one which becomes ours without ceasing to be from heaven'' (*Dictionary of Biblical Theology,* p. 285).

Justice is also seen by Paul as God's great mercy. Because of the sacrifice of Christ, the Father responds with mercy to his sinful children.

If there can be no peace without justice, there can be no justice without love. If we love, we will want to free people from their sins as much as from the hellish cycle of poverty, sexism and other kinds of prejudice.

It is tempting to get on this or that bandwagon, to launch this or that crusade, to join this or that demonstration—but a Christian cannot and must not ever limit his or her witness to the world's agenda. We are about an eternal kingdom which, even if we never fully achieve justice in this life, will surpass anything we can imagine in terms of love, justice and peace.

Now that we have taken a brief look at faith, truth and justice, let's look again at the passage quoted at the beginning of this chapter, Acts 2:40-47. You may want to read it again before continuing here.

Who We Are as Church

This scripture holds the kernel of what and who we are as Church. It can become for us and all generations of Christians the standard by which we judge our effectiveness in being what Jesus wants us to be.

1. The thousands of converts and the disciples remained faithful to the apostles' teaching. The apostles taught one main truth—that Jesus of Nazareth was the Son of God, that he rose from the dead and that he was

coming again. So strong was their conviction that people found themselves making an act of faith in Jesus, requesting baptism and joining the community of faith.

2. There was a strong fellowship in which the people shared everything in common. It was believed in the first few years of the Church that the end times were imminent so there was no need for saving for a rainy day. However, the Christians' motivation to share everything in common was rooted in a more sublime reality. The Holy Spirit enflamed them with such love that no brother or sister was allowed to go in need. Love made them truly one—just as we sometimes find families so in love that everyone pools her and his paycheck for the sake of the entire family.

3. The breaking of the bread was central to the faith of the new Church. The Eucharist was celebrated in the homes and was recognized, even at that early time, as a most sacred way in which to enter into the reality of the passion and death of Jesus.

4. Still regarding themselves as faithful Jews, the Christians continued going to the temple for the Hebrew prayers. They recognized Jesus as the fulfillment of their greatest hopes as Jews. Most Jews, however, did not believe as the Christians did, and this difference finally divided, once for all, the Christians from Judaism. The Christian community continued to be a praying community. There is evidence throughout the Pauline and pastoral letters of a praying people of God.

After several confrontations with Jews who did not accept Christ—and under the growing influence of non-Jewish Christians, the Church in Jerusalem began to realize they were a new chosen people, a people of the New Covenant sealed in the Blood of Christ and called by God to announce the arrival of the Messiah and the salvation of the world.

The faith and love of the disciples were so strong that they won the approval of other people. People looked on them with awe, admiration and maybe a hint of envy. They were so much in love with Jesus, so excited about him and so constant in proclaiming what he had accomplished that they kept "adding to their number."

Today we have our own tensions, trials and failings.

The Church—the People of God—is always striving for perfection. We have to grow together, repent together, constantly measure our spoken faith against God's Word and our lived faith.

It is time, now, for our final reflection in this book, *Do Whatever He Tells You.*

After this final reflection, I have a few parting thoughts that may be helpful to you in your efforts to overcome any habitual sin that makes your life miserable and less effective as a Christian.

For Personal Reflection

Scripture

"We brought nothing into this world, nor have we the power to take anything out. If we have food and clothing we have all that we need. Those who want to be rich are falling into temptation and a trap. They are letting themselves be captured by foolish and harmful desires which drag men down to ruin and destruction. The love of money is the root of all evil. Some men in their passion for it have strayed from the faith, and have come to grief amid great pain.

"Man of God that you are, flee from all this. Instead, seek after integrity, piety, faith, love, steadfastness, and a gentle spirit. Fight the good fight of faith. Take firm hold on the everlasting life to which you were called when, in the presence of many witnesses, you made your profession of faith" (1 Tm. 6:7-12).

Prayer

Lord, I know I am supposed to do my part to alleviate suffering, to overcome injustice, to bring about a balance of power and a sharing of wealth in my own life and in the world at large. Help me overcome my hesitancy to practice faith, hope and love. Make me an image of your own goodness, Jesus, and use me as you will. Every good thing I have comes from you. I now give it back to you to be used as you see fit. Amen.

Examination of Conscience:

You shall not steal.

- Am I grateful to God for my many blessings and do I share them with others?

- Am I aware that everything I have belongs to God and should be used to help those who have less? Do I steal from God and my fellow man by not sharing the gifts God has given me for the sake of others?

- Do I try to influence human events through the ballot, letters to public officials, and prayer?

- Am I active in my parish and do I participate in ministries to the poor and in parish council and other groups that concern themselves with justice issues?

Decision

Here, another two-part decision.

1. To develop a constant awareness that everything I have is a gift from God and that I am called to share with others and respect their rights and property, I will

_____

_____

_____

_____

_____

_____.

2. To assume my share of the responsibilities in my parish and community to insure that the gospel is proclaimed and the Good News preached, I will

_____

_____

_____

_____

_____

_____.

Prayer

In this moment of grace, Jesus, I truly want to live completely for you and for others. Help me to make my time your time, my heart your heart. Amen.

For Shared Reflection

Scripture

"And now, brothers [and sisters], I beg you through the mercy of God to offer your bodies as a living sacrifice holy and acceptable to God, your spiritual worship. Do not conform yourselves to this age but be transformed by the renewal of your mind, so that you may judge what is God's will, what is good, pleasing and perfect" (Rom. 12:1-2).

Prayer

Lord Jesus, we want to be a family of faith, a power for truth, a champion of justice. Fill us with your Spirit and root out from our community all that is carnal, selfish and sinful. Make us a holy people that pleases you through service to others. Amen.

Discussion starters

1. St. Paul tells us that we are to be transformed by the "renewal of our minds." Through renewal, we will be able to decide what is God's will and how to be good and pleasing to him.

• What programs in our parish already help us to become renewed in mind and heart?

• Are there any programs we might suggest to improve our parish ministry for parishioners seeking spiritual growth?

2. True justice seeks the positive good of people and does not only try to free them from oppression. The "positive good" of a person includes a personal relationship with Jesus. The "positive good" of society includes reversing immoral or amoral trends that weaken faith, distance people from God's truth and promote the welfare of the powerful few.

- When we speak of justice in our family, prayer group or parish, just what are we talking about? What has been our understanding of justice in the past? Can it or should it be different in the future?

- How can we support our pastors and parish educators in their efforts to help the parish grow in faith and in effectively reaching out into the secular community?

- Would it be helpful for our parish to reflect, through a retreat or a "town hall meeting" on how well we live up to the call to evangelize and minister to the world?

Decision

To foster a desire for constant spiritual growth in our faith community and to help achieve justice in at least one area of life, we will _____

_____

_____

_____

_____

_____

_____

_____

_____.

Prayer

Lord, at the end of this last reflection in Do Whatever He Tells You, we ask you to help us do what you want done, to please you by obeying you. Through the Holy Spirit, give us the desire and strength to follow through on our decisions to continue to love and serve others, to respect life, to conserve our natural resources and to promote peace.

Thank you for the gift of these reflections, for our growth in love and understanding, for loving us and saving us, for healing us and forgiving us, for calling us and using us.

We are your people.
You are our God.
May you be praised forever.
May our lives proclaim your goodness.
Amen.
Amen.

A Final Word

I hope this book has helped readers discover how they may more easily "smooth out" their journey into the kingdom of God, leveling mountains and filling valleys. Overcoming habitual sin and other problems is possible through the power of Jesus Christ.

There are five key thoughts in this book that we should keep in mind to grow in the love and service of the Lord, to learn more and more how to please him so that we can live in joy.

1. Joy comes from peace; peace comes from faith and trust in God.

2. We are made in the image of God; we are called to be like him; when we are like him we find joy; when we are not like him, we are miserable and spread misery abroad.

3. Jesus wants both to forgive us and to deliver us from evil; we can't overcome sin ourselves, but he can and does as long as we place ourselves in his hands; he delivers us individually and as a Church; remember to be dead to sin (Rom. 6:1ff.).

4. The sacraments are God-with-us; in the sacraments we encounter the living, glorified and powerful

Jesus; we, the Church, are the "eighth sacrament," making him present to all the world.

5. Mary is the Mother of God, Mother of the Church and our Mother; she is the model for all Christians who want to find joy in pleasing God; it is Mary who advises us, "Do whatever he tells you."

I hope that through these pages, you have begun to find more joy by striving to please God more often.

Remember, Jesus loves you. How else could we explain the cross?

God bless you and keep you. Peace be with you. May his favor rest with you and your love with him.

Deacon Henry Libersat
Feast of the Assumption,
August 15, 1989

Sources Quoted

Liturgy of the Hours, Book III, Catholic Book Publishing Company, New York, pages 445; 450-1.

"The Mother of Jesus in Scripture," G. Graystone, M.M., an essay in *A New Catholic Commentary on Holy Scripture*, Thomas Nelson, Inc.

The Gospel of Mark, video by Father Eugene LaVerdiere, S.S., produced by Eternal Word Television Network, Birmingham.

Dictionary of Biblical Theology, edited by Xavier Leon Dufour, page 285, Seabury, New York.

All Scripture quotes taken from *The New American Bible*, Copyright © 1970 by the Confraternity of Christian Doctrine, Washington D.C., are used with permission.

About the Author

Deacon Henry Libersat was born July 4, 1934. He and his wife, Peg, have seven children and twenty grandchildren.

He was ordained to the permanent diaconate for the Diocese of Orlando on Pentecost Sunday, May 18,1986. He holds a masters degree in Pastoral Ministry from St. Thomas University, Miami.

Deacon Henry began a career in the Catholic Press in 1957. He was editor of the Catholic paper for the Diocese of Lafayette in Louisiana, worked for a while at Our Sunday Visitor in Huntington, Indiana, and since 1969 has been editor and manager of *The Florida Catholic*, which serves six of Florida's seven dioceses.

He has won several national journalism awards including the 1988 St. Francis de Sales Award for "Outstanding Contributions to Catholic Journalism," the highest award given to individuals by the Catholic Press Association of the United States and Canada.

He has written extensively for Catholic publications including *Liguorian*, *Our Sunday Visitor*, and *The Family*.

174 DO WHATEVER HE TELLS YOU

Deacon Henry is author of *Ragin' Cajun*, Liguori Publications, 1974; *Caught in the Middle*, Crossroad, 1976; *Way, Truth and Life*, St. Paul Books & Media, 1988. He is co-author with Sister Briege McKenna of the best-selling, *Miracles Do Happen*, Servant Publications, 1986.

He is also author of a 1989 Liguori Publications pamphlet, *Permanent Deacons, Who They Are and What They Do*. Another 1990 book is *Miracle in the Marketplace*, Resurrection Press.

As time permits, Deacon Henry responds to invitations to preach and teach in parishes, retreats and conferences as well as on radio and television programs.